I0072779

Short-Term Rental Success:

Create Welcoming Five Star Stays

Christine D. Shuck

While every precaution has been taken in the preparation of this book, the publisher assumes no responsibility for errors or omissions, or for damages resulting from the use of the information contained herein.

SHORT-TERM RENTAL SUCCESS

First edition. December 1, 2022.

Copyright © 2022 Christine D. Shuck.

ISBN: 978-1955150309

Written by Christine D. Shuck.

Also by Christine D. Shuck

Benton Security Services
Hired Gun
Smoke and Steel

Chronicles of Liv Rowan
Fate's Highway

Gliese 581g
G581: The Departure
G581: Mars
G581: Earth

War's End
War's End: The Storm
War's End: A Brave New World
Tales of the Collapse
War's End Omnibus - Books 1-3

Standalone

The War on Drugs: An Old Wives Tale
Get Organized, Stay Organized
Winter's Child
Short-Term Rental Success

Watch for more at christineshuck.com.

Table of Contents

Preface 1

Part I: Are Short-Term Rentals for You?................................. 7

Do You Have What It Takes?... 9

Successful Hosts Are... 13

Short-Term? Mid-Term? Or Long-Term? 21

How Much Will I Make? 27

Part II: Planning It.. 35

We Can Do Better 37

The Trifecta—Choose Two... 41

Evaluate Your Space... 43

Themes and Décor.. 49

Pets? Yes or No? 57

Children? Yes or No? 65

Rental Insurance.. 67

Anticipating Costs... 73

What Do YOU Expect from Your Guests? 77

Part III: Creating the Perfect Space 79

Preparing the Space 81

Safety and First Aid 93

The Guest Handbook 97

Signs Make the Difference.. 99

Part IV: Bookings, Platforms, Guests 105

Platforms—An Overview 107

Is Booking Direct Right for You? 111

Posting Your Listing on Airbnb 113

Editing and Refining Your Listing on Airbnb 119

Accepting and Welcoming Your First Guests 143

Part V: Become the Host with the Most.. 147

Be a Professional.. 149

Communicate Clearly and Effectively.. 153

Attaining Superhost Status 169

Part VI: Cleaning, Dealing with Reviews, Solving Problems......... 173

Cleaning Your STR - Step-by-Step 175

When Things go South... 187

Reviews, Reviews, Reviews!.. 191

Social Media Presence.. 209

Part VII: Money Matters.. 213

The Art of the Upsell... 215

Top Business Write-Offs for STRs... 223

Keeping Track of Your Financials.. 227

Taxes and Tax Reporting.. 233

Part VIII: A Multitude of Tips.. 237

Buying Tips 239

Beware, Scammers Ahead! 241

Perform Regular Scheduled Maintenance...................... 245

The Art of Home Décor 249

Listen to Your Guests.. 251

How to Identify and Avoid Problem Guests.................. 255

Security Cameras - Do's and Don'ts............................. 261

Maximize Profit Without Being Cheap......................... 265

Embrace Fun 267

Part IX: The Future 271

When to Get Out 273

In Summary... 279

Part X: Additional Resources....................................... 281

STR Co-Host Resources 283

Podcasts and Facebook Groups 285

Additional Reading 287

Part XI: Spreadsheets and Lists 289

Spreadsheets Detailed 291

Shopping/Stocking Lists 303

To my family. Always. You are my everything. And to Dori, Kate and Rachel from ILS. Thanks for allowing me to write instead of diagramming sentences, the creative rebel in me appreciates you more than I can express.

Preface

———

Welcome to *Short-Term Rental Success: Create Welcoming Five Star Stays.*

I am an author and also a rental property owner in Kansas City, Missouri. At present, I own four homes in and around Kansas City. The first is a long-term rental south of Kansas City and the first house I ever owned. The other three are all in a row, on the same street, with our residence right in the middle. After we purchased our 1899 Victorian in Historic Northeast Kansas City in 2013, we rented our first house out as a long-term rental. In 2014, we picked up another house for $25 just at the end of our large yard. The journey from purchase to renovation of that house, which we call Cottage West, is summarized here on our short-term rental website: https://www.thecottagebb.com/storyofcottagewest. It became our first short-term rental in late 2019. We bought a third house on the other side of our property in 2017, which we call Cottage East. It is currently undergoing renovations and will be available as an STR by the end of 2024. We also have two unique STRs, both RV/Campers—the Hedy Lamarr vintage Airstream, which went into service as a short-term rental in 2021 and Proud Mary, a 1969 Holiday Rambler currently being renovated that will be available by mid-2023.

I have a wealth of business experience, specifically that of customer service, in a variety of industries from over twenty years in administrative, help desk, and customer service positions. My experiences in customer service helped me immeasurably when I jumped out of the corporate world and into the entrepreneurial one—first with a cleaning business in 2005, then later as a professional organizer, author, and community educator.

The hospitality business embraces service and professionalism. I have found running an STR to be a perfect position for me. As an introvert, I prefer my exposure to other people to be limited to short bursts of time. And what better way than providing a place for others, where they can check in on their own, but have me close enough to help them should they need anything? It's a win-win for me and my guests!

Throughout this book, I will use a variety of descriptors—*STR, short-term rental, rental property*, even *Airbnb* to describe your property (and mine). The meaning is the same: a property you either own or lease with the purpose of renting out on a short-term basis (anywhere from one night up to six months or more at a time) to guests.

Short-term rentals can also be an excellent way to make a solid income, pay off your mortgage and even jump start other entrepreneurial endeavors. Thanks to the additional income it has brought, I can now work from home, write my books, and build my author business. I am also here for my children when daycare is closed or school isn't in session, and that has been wonderful. We have a grown daughter, a teenager, and our two "littles." We recently adopted our seven-year-old foster daughter and our one-year-old foster son. Having our STRs so close, literally feet away from our home, has meant less expense and less time in just about every way for us.

Perhaps you are looking to make ends meet and put a few dollars in your pocket. Perhaps you are miserable in your day job and want to do something—anything—that differs from the grind of a 9 to 5. You may be a single parent who wants to stay at home with your kids or you may plan to create a rental empire, one property at a time. Do you dream of becoming the owner/manager of two, five, or ten (or more) properties?

You can scale every idea I present up—from one or two, to five, ten properties or more and I'm happy to show you how.

My goal with this book is to help guide you into creating something of unique value for yourself and for the guests that you host. I want you to be successful, and for your guests to leave you messages like these:

I've never been in an Airbnb that was better equipped and organized. We appreciated all the thoughtful touches. - Laurel

SHORT-TERM RENTAL SUCCESS

Christine's home was amazing! Filled with art, books, and thoughtful touches, we could feel that this home was a labor of love! - Danielle

This was the most amazing time! I thank you for sharing your space, your warmth, and your energy with us! I could not have asked for better hosts! - Valencia

I cannot say enough amazing things about this beautiful home. Everything was so thoughtful, from the personal notes placed throughout the house, to the notebook detailing the journey of love put into rehabilitating this home, to the grounds themselves. If I could give it 10 stars, I would. - Sarah

I love your place and if I had an Airbnb, it would be just like yours!... Our other stays on this trip would have been better if they had notes like yours (and if they had been as clean as yours). - Martene

These reviews don't get old, not at all. You will see plenty more throughout the book. The feedback from so many happy guests made me realize that, 1) I had tapped in to what made guests happy, and 2) I should share that with others.

My personal experiences are solely in long-term rentals and short-term rentals of properties separate from, yet next to, my home. And I'm going to focus on this specific area—short-term rentals where the guests have the entire place to themselves—rather than branching out into areas I know little about. But even if you intend to use rental arbitrage, or share your home by renting out a room or two, I think you will find my book helpful.

By the end of this book, you should have an excellent grasp of short-term rentals and how to create a space that is welcoming, hospitable and encourages repeat business. I will touch on financial concerns, planning for the unexpected, must haves for every STR, the proper mindset, and more. There are plenty of lists—everything you need to stock each room in your unit, thoughtful additional touches, a cleaning supplies list (I was a professional house cleaner for over fifteen years) and step-by-step cleaning advice.

I will cover handling problem guests and techniques for dealing with them, what wording you can use to get excellent reviews, how to respond (or not) to poor reviews, outsourcing your cleanings (or how to clean a property properly yourself). We will even touch on the art of the up-sell.

I will give you some good reasons to list your property not just on the behemoth company of Airbnb, but also on VRBO and others, as well as how you may wish to go about accepting direct bookings. There are pros and cons, and I will discuss them in as much detail as possible.

I hope to impart to you a combination of humanity and business ethic that is so necessary to becoming a successful short-term rental owner and host. With kindness and compassion, with clear rules and expectations, you can run a successful, lucrative short-term rental out of your shared space or separate property. And you can also craft a property that earns gushing reviews like this one:

Here's what Kathleen wrote

Kathleen

We were floored by the care, consideration, and thoughtfulness that Christine put into the cottage Staying here made us feel like a part of her and her family's Airbnb adventure It is easy to see that Christine, Dave, and family are making a true difference in the rebound of their neighborhood. The house was plenty spacious and oh so adorable We did not want for anything during our stay Having off street and gated parking was also a plus Everywhere we wanted to explore, eat, or drink was all within an easy, short drive We hope to return and stay longer the next time we visit Kansas City!

Kathleen's private feedback for you:

"Thank you for hosting us. We hope to return to your cute cottage."

Nice, isn't it? I get reviews like this regularly. By the end of this book, you will be ready to open your own short-term rental business and welcome your first guests. Welcome to *Short-Term Rental Success*!

Part I: Are Short-Term Rentals for You?

———

Do You Have What It Takes?

———

D o you have what it takes to operate a short-term rental property? That's a very realistic question to ask yourself. Because it absolutely is not for everyone.

I'm going to list off some qualities in hosts that I have found essential to success in the short-term rental business in the next chapter, but before I do, I'm going to be blunt.

If you are looking for a get rich quick situation with zero work involved, this is not the business venture for you.

I work approximately thirty hours a month and gross over $6,100 on our three properties (one long-term rental, two short-term rental). But it took a long time, thousands of dollars, and lots of planning and learning to get there. I had weeks, months even, of planning and hard work as we renovated our property and I read books, listened to hundreds of hours of podcasts, and made extensive lists of what my property needed to be a success. There was also a rather inconvenient pandemic right at the beginning of our STR adventures that really hit our finances hard. It is only now, after three years and two STR properties, that I have that income, income that should more than double once our other two STR properties are up and running. And to be honest, I'm on the low end of the earning spectrum because of my location. I specialize in providing excellent hospitality at a cheap price.

While in some ways you can set it all in place and then sit back and earn money, that's also an incredibly limited way of thinking. Running an STR requires constant upkeep and improvement. It requires learning what your guests are looking for and making sure it is there waiting for them. An STR operator must provide service, cleanliness and a professional, courteous response each time, every time, without fail. You don't get to take sick days, or vacation, unless you outsource the management and cleaning of it.

Providing a short-term rental means you are in the hospitality business. Are you *hospitable*? Are you *professional* in your communications and responses? Can you be *patient* with what might seem like endless questions? Can you deal with guests who don't read your rules and then ask you all the questions that were answered in the handbook? In the middle of winter, when your guest can't see where the driveway ends and drives off of it and gets stuck in the snow, are you ready to dig them out? Or call a tow truck? When a light bulb burns out in the bathroom, can you get over with a new one and troubleshoot a variety of issues with patience and grace?

You don't get to be short-tempered, pissy, or snide. You don't get to assume a guest "should know better."

Well, honestly, you *can* be all of those things. Plenty of hosts are. I see their posts every day on the Facebook groups I'm in. They are petty, cheap, and small-minded. They are penny wise and pound foolish.

Sure, you can pinch pennies and cut corners. You can set out one roll of thin, one-ply toilet paper and tell a guest to "go buy more at the store" if you like. But the reviews from your guests will reflect your unwillingness to provide hospitable service.

"But wait!" you might say to me, "Didn't Airbnb start with a couple of air mattresses on the floor?" Yes, it did. But just as with everything else in life, it grew, and it evolved. Go to the Airbnb website and look around. What do you see? Do you see plain air mattresses on the floor? The bare bones? No, you don't. Not anymore. You see carefully curated photos, amazing destinations, cool places to stay. Clean lines. Thoughtful spaces. You will not be a successful STR host if you don't grow and change with the industry.

My point in all of this is that being in the hospitality industry takes a very specific mindset. It doesn't mean kissing a guest's ass, instead it means patience, understanding, clarity, *more* patience, and avoiding giving your guests a piece of your mind when things go awry. When problems arise, what you say, and *how you say it*, can make all the difference in the world. I'll get into more specifics later on this.

Operating an STR is not for everyone. And you might discover it is not for you as you make your way through this book. If that is the case, it's still a win. You will learn you are not cut out for it and you will have paid a small price (the price of this book) to learn a valuable lesson. Better to pay $6.99 on an ebook than spend thousands of dollars readying your first short-term rental, only to find out you are in the wrong business.

Next up? Read on to learn more about what successful hosts do to keep their ratings high and their guests happy.

Successful Hosts Are...

―――

"*I just don't understand how you guys are making so much money with Airbnb. I hated my guests. They were all pains in the ass.*" - A neighbor who briefly ran a short-term rental out of his home.

I'm going to give you the number one tip for successful hosting. A successful host sets their ego aside. If you don't, you will be like our friend quoted above, convinced of his own perfection and pissed off anytime he received a negative review (even when the guests kept the feedback private).

Who are successful hosts? What do they look like? What do their properties look like? How did they get to where they are now?

Successful hosts anticipate the needs of their guests and keep their prices competitive. Their rentals are unique, well-stocked, and so much more. You don't have to be each of these things all the time. You don't have to aim for perfection out of the gate, but you need to learn. Not just from the lists below, but in the first days, weeks and months after you open your own STR.

No matter how much you plan, how many books you read on the subject, or how many podcasts you listen to, nothing will adequately prepare you for the reality of it all. And you will learn. Oh, how you will learn! Look at what I, and many others, have learned along the way, but be prepared for your own learning curve. I asked myself (and Google), "What are the hallmarks of a successful host" and the answers to that question are below.

Let's look at what successful hosts do and who they are. Successful hosts...

Do their research—Look at who the top-performing STRs are on the various rental sites. The big ones, Airbnb and VRBO, are especially important. The first three pages of results for your area are the places you want to emulate or beat in terms of appearance and amenities. Look for properties that closely match your own if you already have a place in mind. (i.e., if you have a two-bedroom one bath apartment, look at the description, pricing, and amenities offered). Take your time, read the descriptions, take notes on what stands out, and think about what you might do differently based on the information presented. How does the host present the property? How can you do it better?

Doing your research will give you a good idea of how much you can charge for your own property.

Demonstrate creativity—What others are doing? Provide something more, something different, or unique that will draw guests' attention. I noticed a lot of beige or even plain white walls in listings when I was still in the planning stages of my STR. In town for a conference, I had recently stayed at Gimpy's, an adorable Airbnb outside of Franklin, Tennessee (shown later) and beige and white were the antithesis of what I hoped to provide. I wanted color and comfort, books, and art. And I banked (rather successfully, I might add) on my future guests wanting it too.

Provide empathy—Even when it is totally the guest's fault, show empathy and it can go very far. Did your guest miscalculate how long it would take to drive cross-country and arrived in the wee hours of the morning on a one-night stay? Give them an extra hour to check out. Commiserate with them. Be *human*. We are in the hospitality business and kindness goes a long way.

Are thorough—The details are so important. They will, in fact, make or break your success as an STR. Take the time to make a lot of lists, or use the lists provided here in this book. Make a checklist of must-haves that you want to provide with your STR. Take your time, look it over multiple times, then figure out a way to keep these things stocked. I take inventory every six months. I also replenish some items (toilet paper, paper towels, Kleenex, analgesics) at every cleaning. Others may be more of a monthly thing. And it isn't just being stocked that is important, but that you examine things like the messages you send (I highly recommend setting up automated messages, more on that later) and what details they include.

A successful host looks at every detail of a guest's stay—from accepting their request, to welcoming and hosting them, to cleaning up and preparing for the next guest. The entire experience should be seamless and easy for the guest and for you.

Have objectivity—Whether you are assessing a property for viability as an STR or rolling with the punches of a critical review, the ability to stay objective will help immeasurably. It's tough when someone gives you a critical review, and you also might be blind to a serious issue with the property you are hoping to rent out. Getting others to provide input can really help.

Are optimistic with a healthy dose of self-discipline—Even when finances dip, and they will, you stay focused on the future. Here in Kansas City, I look forward to the busy season (May through August), and I have learned to plan the fix-it projects for when things are slow. And after the COVID pandemic, I learned for a fact that even in the busy season, business can hit rock bottom. When the money is flying in, it can be quite a rush. That said, there will be down-time, time you need to bite the bullet and close for unexpected repairs (even if you don't own the property). Be optimistic, but have an emergency fund handy!

Are accountable—Be responsible, take accountability, be a professional to the guest. If a cleaning is not up to snuff, own it, even if you hired it out to someone else. Offer to fix it immediately. Did your listing state you had separate dishes for kids and they aren't there? Go get it and bring it to them.

Focus on customer service—What makes a great experience for a guest? A host who cares about their comfort and happiness. Anticipate your guest's needs. I have labeled every drawer and cabinet clearly to make it easy to find things. Have tampons, pads, toothbrushes, analgesics and more on hand—your guests will be grateful for them when they have the unexpected happen.

Learn from early mistakes—You will make them. Mistakes are inevitable. That said, you can learn from them and that changes them from *mistakes* into *learning opportunities.*

Set a fair price—Sure, everyone wants to charge (and get) the best price possible, but if you can find a middle ground, one that is at a more reasonable amount, you may find that when problems arise, your guests are more likely to give you a little grace. Not always, but enough for it to make the difference.

Are as flexible as possible—How can you be more flexible? Consider the following areas:

- A shorter minimum stay—I've had amazing luck with the one-night minimum stay, but that is because I am close, and I'm handling the cleanings myself). Figure out what works best for you but offer the as many choices as possible.

- More flexible check in times—My checkout time is 11 a.m. and my check-in time is 2 p.m., but I try to allow for early check-ins and late check-outs)

- Allow for self-check-in—I've encountered hosts that insist on being there to greet me when I arrive. That can be nice, but it can also be awkward, or downright inconvenient if I'm not running on time.

- Accommodate an extra guest—I've seen guests who nervously ask if it is okay to have an additional guest over. Mind you, we aren't talking about twenty extra guests, a mariachi band and a full-blown party, just one or two more than what they mentioned upon booking. Unless you have an additional per guest fee in place (which I discourage, since it makes liars out of otherwise honest people), then let it go. I'm cleaning the entire place after a guest departs, so one or two extra truly doesn't make a difference.

Update their property photos regularly—I cannot emphasize how important this is. Set a reminder to do these every six months or after any major change in furniture. Otherwise, you will get dinged on the Accuracy rating on Airbnb and other platforms. Even if they are improvements, folks want what they have seen in the photos, otherwise they fall to their rampant fears of being scammed by a host. Accuracy is so very important! More on this later.

Start off on the right foot with guests—You are in the hospitality business. Your guests' needs are your priority.

- Ask them what they need (food/activity recommendations)

- Give them easy-to-follow directions and check-in instructions

- Make sure they can easily access any needed items (use labels, notes, etc.)

Vet their guests—Vetting guests is so important, especially when you are newly open for business. When you are new, that's when the locals and scammers target you. They are actually looking for listings that have few or no reviews—because they are running a scam, or because they want to throw a raging party. Your job is to handpick your first twenty to fifty guests and establish yourself with an abundance of five-star ratings. After that, the flood of ne'er-do-wells subsides.

- Ask a question like "What brings you to our area?" and this encourages a potential guest to give you information like "I'm coming to town for a conference" etc.

- Examine a guest's profile—are they new to the platform, are they local, do they have any other reviews, and if so, what do the reviews say?

- Guests often include a message even if not prompted. "I'm coming in for a wedding" or "I'm in town for a Chief's game" are good ones.

- Avoid locals (especially at the beginning; again, you are a target) unless they have a decent list of positive reviews. I have occasionally broken this rule, and around 30% of the time I've regretted it.

Are well-spoken (and well-written)—Words are important, folks. And not just for writers like me. How you speak (or write) and what you say, and the tone in which you say it, are so very important. You are giving a lot away by how you write/speak. Your education level, your personality, and so much more shows in the words you choose and the tone you write them in. Take the time to set up automated messages and templates on the various hosting platforms so that you can hone your information and instructions into as concise, clear, and judgment-free of language as possible. If English is your second language, or wasn't your strongest subject in school, consider asking someone else for help in constructing clear, concise, well-worded messages for your guests.

Well organized—Successful hosts are organized financially and logistically. You will find sample, bare bones spreadsheets and shopping/stocking lists for your STR, later in this book. They are all easy to adapt to your own uses. A successful host plans for unexpected expenses (HVAC repairs, damages, etc.) and has an amount of money set aside for emergencies. They plan for regular maintenance, maintain all supplies necessary for the smooth functioning of their STR, and have an actionable "to do" list constantly updated.

Are thoughtful—Not only does a successful host anticipate their guests' needs, they also learn and improve with each challenging experience. A guest is also far more willing to forgive a misstep if they have ample proof of how important their happiness is to their host. Think about what *you* want or need while traveling to a strange city. What might you forget? What would you be thankful for a host to provide to you?

Remain open to criticism—Hosts recognize that no matter how perfect an experience they provide, there will be feedback that they can learn from and used to provide a better experience with each guest after.

Are business minded—Despite maintaining a strong hospitable, customer-service oriented ethic, successful hosts are also aware of the bottom line. They don't hand out discounts right and left and they have a clear set of boundaries and rules.

Remain accommodating and hospitable (even when guests are a pain in the patoot)—Guests can often challenge hosts. A successful host knows how to rise above a needy or confrontational guest and still provide the best stay possible.

Maintain good neighbor relationships—Recognizing that our neighbors' needs and opinions can often be essential to our success, excellent hosts are respectful of their neighbors and try to create (and maintain) positive relationships with them.

Offer a Curated Experience—Figure out what our guests need and then provide it to them. Whether it is gluten-free dining, local art museums, or pet-friendly destinations—a successful host has their finger on the pulse of the city or town their STR is in.

We will go into many of these areas in more detail in the pages to come. Next, we are going to discuss what length of stay you are hoping to host your guests for.

Short-Term? Mid-Term? Or Long-Term?

———

Even with an STR, there is some wiggle room when allowing for a minimum to maximum stay. To clarify, in the short-term rental world, when we speak of short-term, mid-term and long-term guests, we can categorize them this way:

- Short-term STR: 1 day to 1 week

- Mid-term STR: 1-3 weeks

- Long-term STR: 30-90 days

What do you prefer? Do you want only short-term guests? Mid-term? Or are you interested in long-term guests?

It's difficult to predict the exact guest that will find your place appealing, but that answer will pretty quickly resolve once you have opened for business. As my husband and I were putting the finishing touches on Cottage West, our first STR, I envisioned it as an artist's and writer's retreat. I knew we were just moments away from a major highway hub, and that our central location made it perfect for guests to jump on and off the highway easily, but I vastly underestimated the amount of one-night stays we would receive. Now I embrace it. And because I handle my own cleanings, except while on vacation, that is a significant amount of income that stays in my pocket.

Things to consider when deciding what length of stay is for you might include:

- Cleaning fees

- Proximity

- Involvement

- Risk

Cleaning fees—For Cottage West, approximately 90% of our guests stay for one night. A few stay for a weekend, even fewer still for up to five days, and I don't see many requests for longer stays. For me, that's fine. It's hard to make a place dirty when you only stay one night, so I earn bank on cleaning fees! And considering that I handle all the cleanings and live right next door, a solid 40% of our monthly income is from the cleaning fees. We charge $50 in cleaning fees for a one-night stay and $60 for a stay lasting longer than two days. I take around 45 minutes to clean Cottage West. Yes, that means I'm cleaning it up to seven days a week, but since it is right next door to me, and I work from home, that's super-easy!

You may prefer longer stays. Maybe you work full time and need to hire out the cleanings, maybe you travel, or maybe cleaning an STR daily is the last thing you want to deal with. Brief stays equal less mess but potentially more time out of your week turning things over or arranging for a cleaner to do the work for you. Mid-term, where guests stay anywhere from one to three weeks might be more your style.

Proximity—Your proximity to the property, or your ability to find others to manage the property for you, will affect the decisions you make on whether to offer reduced rates for longer-term stays.

Proximity to your property can be a major influence on what bookings you require. I will admit that I'm a bit of a control freak. I can't imagine owning an out of town or out-of-state STR. Then again, I will never be an owner who has a dozen or more properties. I far prefer to provide a personal, hands-on experience for my guests.

As I mentioned above, cleaning fees, especially if you are doing the cleanings yourself, can be a lovely bonus income. And this is, of course, tied to your proximity to and involvement in the STR you own. Not sure you can clean a place quickly and efficiently, or up to your guests' standards? Don't worry, I will cover that later.

Involvement—How involved will you be in the day-to-day operations of your STR? In my case, I handle pretty much everything except performing the big maintenance. I handle most of the guest interactions (I leave the specific brewery and sometimes dining recommendations to my husband); track income and expense and adjust the nightly fees in order to increase occupancy and income. I clean the property, handle painting, plan improvements, and schedule repairs. As you can see, I'm *very* involved. I also don't work a job outside of the home. It helps that we live next door to our STR properties, making it incredibly easy for me to handle these tasks.

Perhaps you work a steady nine-to-five job. Perhaps you live across town, or you suck at cleaning. It's okay—not everyone is cut out to do it—but in case you want to learn how, I've added detailed advice on cleaning your STR later in the book.

I believe it is better to be more involved at first, and slowly farm out the work to others as time goes by. After all, if you are running the day-to-day operations yourself, you know exactly what you need from others and can give them this information when they work for you. You will know how important a good response time is, what a truly clean STR looks like (again, I'll discuss this later in the book) and what you should stock it with. You will have worked out most of the hiccups and weirdness. And believe me, no matter how many details I give you, there will be situations I haven't covered, and you will encounter them and learn from them. Finally, the length of stay can affect your involvement. If you are working full time and looking for longer stays where you don't need to be at the property often, then a longer stay would be quite attractive to you because there's less to do on a day-to-day basis. There is one other thing to consider.

Risk—It can vary depending on what part of the United States (or world) you are in, but most times, once a guest crosses the 30 days mark for occupancy, it may entitle them to certain protections under local housing laws. There are a few areas in the United States where guests are *automatically conferred rights as tenants no matter how short of a time they stay* and I urge you to be very careful in those areas. Once a guest has rights as a tenant, either right away in those few areas, or after 28 to 30 days of occupancy, it can be extremely difficult to remove them from your property. You can mitigate these risks by requiring a guest to sign a rental contract with you in situations where they might stay long enough to qualify as a resident, but it won't eliminate that risk entirely. If they violated their contract, you will still need to sue them in court.

Keep these in mind as you continue to plan and roll out your STR property. Much of this might depend as well on the guests you can expect to have. Join, if you haven't already, several STR groups in your area. You can usually find them on Facebook by searching for "Airbnb" or "VRBO" or "short-term rentals" or "STR." These groups, especially local host groups, can help you in a variety of ways, up to and including identifying the perfect length of stay for your STR. I have listed the links to many of the ones I belong to under *Part X: Podcasts and Facebook Groups*.

Wear and tear—I see many people in the Facebook host groups who say they avoid 100% occupancy because of the "wear and tear." I profoundly disagree with this statement based on my own experiences as both an STR host and a LTR landlord.

The best way to avoid wear and tear would be to only rent your STR for one-night stays. Frankly, with one night, and the proper screening in place (no locals!), your guests rarely have the opportunity to create wear and tear. Give them a few days, a week, a month or more, and be damned if they won't do some damage!

My worst stories come from my long-term rental, where renters have let their dogs eat the trim, broken holes in doors, stopped up plumbing, and not cleaned for their entire tenancy. My next-to-worst stories have come from locals who stayed a few days at a time, with one set breaking two new knives trying to dig their way into 100+ year old door trim to break into the basement and steal the copper (joke was on them—even if they had gotten through, we did everything in Pex).

My point is this: There is only one time a one-night stay caused me any difficulty at all. And it didn't even qualify for "wear and tear." When considering how often you will host guests, please mark "wear and tear" off the list when considering the shortest of stays—one night. Most likely, they will arrive late and leave early and barely touch the amenities.

Let's move on to the burning question. How much will you make?

How Much Will I Make?

———

That is the question you have been dying to know, right? And it is important to answer. After all, you need to have some basic figures in place to know if this is worth your time. Just because the STR market is hot, it doesn't mean it is worth the time and effort, but with some ballpark rates, you can make an educated guess on income.

I remember way back in 2015 being agog over the thought of earning $1,500 a month on a short-term rental. Especially when the low, low rental rates around me meant I would only gross $600 per month on our two-bedroom house if I rented it out as a long-term rental (and still be on the hook for repairs and maintenance). And while rents have grown dramatically since then, I still live in one of the least expensive real estate markets in the United States.

I truly had no inkling of what was possible, but after nearly three years of tracking, I can give you a far better idea. Keep in mind that my property is, once again, in one of the least expensive real estate markets in the country. I also operate on the low end. I prefer my properties booked as close to 100% of the time for a slightly lower rate, while over-delivering on value (better reviews, better future income earning potential).

However, the steps below should give you a basic idea of how to calculate your own potential income.

Start by going to Airbnb.com and type your city and state into the search bar. Narrow down as much as possible to the area that is closest to you. Make sure you are locating comparable properties (same number of bedrooms, for example). Take your time, look at the pictures, note the amenities listed, and how the property looks compared to yours. Try to find at least five that are close to your own in appearance, size, and amenities.

Then fill in the blanks below:

What are the daily, weekend, and cleaning rates in your area for comparable properties?

Comparable Property #1:

Weekday rates:

Weekend rates:

Cleaning fee:

Total cost for a weekday stay:

Total cost for a weekend stay:

Comp Property #2:

Weekday rates:

Weekend rates:

Cleaning fee:

Total cost for a weekday stay:

Total cost for a weekend stay:

Comp Property #3:

Weekday rates:

Weekend rates:

Cleaning fee:

Total cost for a weekday stay:

Total cost for a weekend stay:

Comp Property #4:

Weekday rates:

Weekend rates:

Cleaning fee:

Total cost for a weekday stay:

Total cost for a weekend stay:

Comp Property #5:

Weekday rates:

Weekend rates:

Cleaning fee:

Total cost for a weekday stay:

Total cost for a weekend stay:

Avg weekday rate: (add all 5, then divide by 5)

Avg Weekend rate: (add all 5, then divide by 5)

Avg Cleaning Fee: (add all 5, then divide by 5)

You might also want to compare booking sites. Are the rates the same for the same properties through VRBO? I keep my rates steady at the other sites and only adjust the Airbnb rates. Airbnb is the biggest platform in our area and also the one I do most of my business on, but VRBO and other platforms are slowly, and steadily, growing in momentum. As the largest booking platform, it makes sense for me to adjust my rates on Airbnb if I find I have vacancies less than one week out on my properties.

Here are the 2022 average nightly/cleaning rates below for Cottage West as an example.

Average weekday rate: $75.45 (compared to $69.71 in 2021)

Average weekend rate: $95.09 (compared to $83.35 in 2021)

Cleaning Fees: $50 for 2 days or less, $65 for 3+ day stays

Based on my tracking over the past three years, I know that Cottage West will:

- Have an average occupancy rate of at least 83.75%

- Earn an occupancy rate of at least $82.68 per night

- Earn an overall gross occupancy income of around $25,000 per year

- Earn cleaning fees of at least $10,500 per year (that I get to keep since I do the cleanings)

- Until I pay my mortgage off, it will earn me a gross of $35k per year. After that, at least $42k, likely more, as daily rates will have increased by then.

Once your STR is up and running, the average occupancy rate is typically right around 80%. This varies widely depending on your area, tourism, and seasons. For our Cottage West STR, I know from tracking it I can expect anywhere between 81% and 91% occupancy. In 2021, it was 91% booked for the year. In 2022, that amount fell to just under 84%, but my average occupancy income rose from $73.83 to $82.68 per night.

Factors that may affect your booking rate, and the amount you can charge nightly, include: economy, geopolitical events, and seasonal/weather changes.

This income, depending on where you are located, might appear small, but when compared to an average gross long-term rental income in my area of approximately $900 per month, it makes sense. In the end, I'm earning a gross $35k a year instead of $10,800 in traditional rental income. That's well worth 30 hours of work per month.

I would like to point out that I've accumulated over 500 reviews and had Cottage West in operation for three years at the time of this writing. New properties cannot expect an 80% or higher occupancy rate right out of the gate. It takes time, and it takes reviews and word of mouth and experience before you can expect higher occupancy rates. I highly recommend using projections that include a 45% occupancy rate so that you have worst-case scenarios on hand. Assume and budget for worst case, and you can build up from there.

You can download the spreadsheet I used to track the average daily income and enter and adjust it to fit your needs by going to my author website for your free download: https://www.christineshuck.com/str-success-resources.

Once you have a ballpark on the average nightly rate and cleaning rates, it's time to construct the other half of the equation, your expenses. Once again, do a little research. Reach out to friends/other hosts with same-size properties to anticipate more clearly the utility costs for your particular property.

Here are the 2021 average monthly expenses for Cottage West:

Mortgage:	$505.00
Internet:	$70.00
Electric:	$125.50
Gas:	$53.78
Water:	$67.35
Cell Phone:	$121.10
Repairs/Maintenance:	$67.27
Cleaning Costs:	*$28.33
Property Taxes:	$35.05
Licensing:	$22.63
Security (Ring membership):	$8.33
Accounting (Quicken):	$8.67
Supplies:	$63.00
Streaming services:	$33.00

Total Average Monthly Expenses: $1,209.01

* I handle all the cleanings. The only time I outsource them is when my family and I take our annual vacation, so the $28.33 is actually $340.00 in costs paid over ten days' time.

Average Income: $2,818.47
Average Expenses: $1,209.01
Average Net Income: $1,609.46

In an area where our two-bedroom, one-bath house would rent for a max of $874 per month, choosing to STR it makes sense. I'm doubling my potential income, even after expenses. And don't forget, it is a mere 150 feet away from my home, in eyesight.

Another thing to note—the costs for our internet, cell phones, security, accounting, and streaming services are unchanged when adding another STR to the mix AND we get access to all of those free, so when we added on the Hedy Lamarr Airstream in mid-2021, and plan to add on more, our costs didn't go up in those areas (with few exceptions), making our monthly average expenses lower overall.

I can expect an average net income of around $3,645 per month on our two STRs. Cottage West and the Hedy Lamarr Airstream incomes have grown since last year and are now grossing an average of $4,448.91 per month. I immediately set aside 15% (average of $657.17 per month) of that amount into an interest bearing savings account for unexpected repairs, downtime, and taxes. I also pay myself a salary of $3,000 per month and put any remaining funds left after expenses into a renovations fund for our next to STR projects.

Having this income allows me to 1) stay home and write my books, and 2) be a mom to my kiddos. Later, once our renovation of Cottage East and a second RV are done, and the properties are earning income, we can begin super-paying on our mortgage, eliminating all debt, and building our savings.

In the bigger scheme of things, our combined three house property with yard and two RVs (for four STRs once complete) are small potatoes compared to others on the market. But actually, that is one reason I wrote this book. You don't have to be big. You can stay small, and earn a decent income, while managing one, or a handful, of STRs all on your own.

Keep reading, we have a lot to cover!

Part II: Planning It

We Can Do Better

———

The first year we were in business, we learned so many lessons, and all of them (and more) are right here, for you!

One of the biggest lessons I learned was the host I wanted to be. While I wanted to give my guests space and privacy, I also wanted to be that special host that anticipates every one of my guest's needs and has it ready for them when and if they require it.

You could consider it the golden rule of business—I was hoping to provide the same short-term rental as what I hoped to visit. A place where I could be comfortable, and when the inevitable allergy attack came on, my ears itched for a Q-Tip, my stomach desperately needed an antacid after all of that wonderful fried food I over-indulged in, or I forgot my doggone toothbrush *again*, I was going to reach into the medicine cabinet and find just what I needed. That when I burned or cut myself cooking dinner, I'd find burn gel or a Band-Aid ready to go, right where I needed it. The blankets would be soft, the basic herbs and spices and kitchenware provided, decent coffee (no K-cups, gross!), all of it, in my home away from home.

I wanted convenience and simplicity. I wanted quick results. Above all, I wanted to be left to my own devices and not have to reach out to my host for basic info.

When I travel, I'll open cabinets in order to find what I need if I have to, but I'd far rather someone *label* that cabinet and door, so I can quickly find what I need. Why should I have to search?

I want a good price, comfortable beds, clean rooms, and thoughtful touches. Who doesn't?

If this all seems incredibly complicated, it really isn't. I'll show you how later, but lists help, and frankly, the extra effort in the beginning pays off loads in guest satisfaction and is easy to keep up in the end. Seriously, only one hour a day is spent cleaning and maintaining my STRs. Stick with me—I'll show you exactly how I did it!

We have a unique opportunity with short-term rentals. We can create a beautiful, welcoming environment where someone walks in and feels at home. Some place *better* than home, with their every need anticipated.

We can do better than hotels.

We can even do better than a bed-and-breakfast.

Creating the perfect short-term rental means giving people everything they need and then stepping out of the way, so that they can feel at home in the space you have provided, whether it is for a day, week, month or longer.

We can straddle the line between guest autonomy and 5-star service. And we can do it with style and grace.

Yes, you can also do the bare minimum. You don't have to take on every suggestion I will list in the pages to come. In fact, many STR hosts *don't* do these things and they still make money, and plenty of it. Provide what a hotel provides and you can easily make far more money than you would with a long-term rental. It's true!

What I'm suggesting, however, is a far more radical approach. Yes, there is a place for the standard "kind of like a hotel only an individual owns it" scenario, but there's also a yearning for difference, for a unique stay that moves people to tell their family, their friends, their co-workers "I stayed in this AMAZING cottage on my vacation, the hosts thought of everything and I felt at home there." Or "I was expecting the same old thing, but cheaper than a hotel, and instead it felt like I was *home*." Or even, "Oh my God, I stayed in this adorable little Airstream last weekend! I was in the middle of the city, but it felt like an oasis of green and flowers and it was just... *beautiful*!"

When we travel, we want adventure, quirkiness, color, comfort, and welcoming attitudes. In most cases, it never feels quite like home. The sterility of a hotel room, the starched sheets, the lackluster art, the sameness of one room to another. It is one reason I fell in love with the idea of STRs. Thanks to unique and forward-thinking hosts, I have stayed in some amazing, unique places. And so can you!

My goal when creating our properties was to give the guest an experience which mimicked home enough (or a great experience glamping, with our Airstream) that the guest would never want to leave.

How many times have I heard, "Your place is amazing. When I return to Kansas City, I want to stay here again!"

And while not every single person is going to say that to me, or feel that way, a lot of them do. In fact, *most* of them do. And that is a powerful memory in a guest's mind. They are going to talk about it amongst themselves, with family, friends, and co-workers. They are going to recommend our place to others.

We offer a unique stay, one in which the guest has everything they need to make their stay comfortable, and typically hands-off approach where guests are autonomous (shared spaces are different and we will discuss those differences later), and a place with great service and host responsiveness.

We can also do better from a business and hospitality perspective. I worked for over two decades in a variety of businesses, and it taught me so much. It taught me to give a level of service that I would want to have and to do it without letting guests run roughshod over me.

With a little preparation and understanding, you can do better than others at communication while still clearly managing expectations. Both on the guest's side of things and on your own.

Last, we can do better starting out of the gate, and not repeat the mistakes of others, by reading (and listening to) the tips and tricks of those who have gone before us. I learned so much from podcasts like *Shampoo and Booze* and *Get Paid for Your Pad*. I learned even more about the host I didn't want to be by joining a couple of Facebook groups for short-term rental hosts. By reading what others have done and experienced, you can learn from them and avoid the pitfalls while rising to the top faster and easier than we did.

If all of that sounds like your cup of tea, then read on and remember...

We can do better!

The Trifecta—Choose Two...

M y husband is fond of mentioning that with business, you get to choose one, or even two, but you cannot be all three. What are they?

- You can be the first

- You can be the best/unique/most different

- You can be the cheapest

In my case, I chose the second two. As you will learn as we dig in to this book, I don't live in the best neighborhood. I don't live in the worst, either. Ours is a historic, working-class neighborhood. Each block is different in terms of cleanliness and crime. I accept this. I love living here and have since early 2013 when we moved from a quiet suburb south of Kansas City to one of the oldest residential neighborhoods in Kansas City, now an area euphemistically referred to as "in transition."

Back to the trifecta. I chose to be the best and the cheapest. I think I need to clarify that this doesn't mean the *cheapest* rental out there, but more the *cheapest for the value given.* With our proximity to the highway, we are in a prime location for travelers. Most are driving from one coast to the other and Kansas City is merely a brief stop along the way. We get tourists, and folks interested in staying for a few days, or attending a local Chiefs or Royals game, but most stay for one night and are just looking for a decent place to lay their head down for the night. I keep our prices low, sometimes as low as $51 a night, with a max of $105 per night on the weekends, and I try to give folks the best quality stay that I can provide.

They might just be looking for a place to lay their head down, but I do my best to over-deliver by anticipating every potential need they might have. More on that later. In most cases, I try to be the best by providing a quality place to stay. Perhaps you will be the first to offer a hot tub, or a unique stay like an Airstream, treehouse or Gypsy wagon.

What will make your place unique? What will make it stand out from the rest? More on that later, but for now, I hope I have planted a seed of thought. You can be the first, you can be the best/unique/most different, or you can be the cheapest. But not all three. Which appeal most to you? What can *you* provide that will over-deliver on your guests' expectations?

Evaluate Your Space

———

Perhaps you already have your property and you are ready to get started. Great! Skip ahead to the ideal guest section below. If you are still in the finding a place stage, then let us start with choosing the property you are thinking of. Do you have a specific property in mind? And how is it structured?

Location and Attractions

What are you close to? The airport? A major highway hub? The beach? Mountains? Ski resort? Where you are determines so much. And you need to know all about it so that you can promote it. Make a list of positives; you will use this when you craft your listing. If you are close to a theme park, the waterfront, touristy destinations, conference center, or speedway, write it down. This will come in handy later.

Who is Your Ideal Guest?

Recognize that you can change on this. I originally envisioned hosting writers and readers, but I found I was hosting a high number of one-night stays because of our geographic location. Over 95% of our guests are traveling through from one coast to the other.

Child and/or Infant Friendly?

Unless you are planning on an upscale, exclusive resort-style destination, I'm going to suggest that you remain child/infant friendly. Families travel and they especially appreciate STRs over hotels and motels because of the obvious benefits provided (kitchens, bedrooms, and often more). Child/infant friendly means including a pack 'n play, high chair, and possibly other child/infant-centric items such as:

- Games/puzzles/toys

- Art supplies (coloring books, crayons, or colored pencils)

- Outlet covers

- Plastic dishware and utensils

They don't take up a lot of space, and families with young children deeply appreciate not having to tote the items in with them.

Pet-Friendly or Not?

Deciding on whether to allow pets can be a difficult one. You never know exactly what other pet owners find acceptable until they visit with their animals.

All of my properties are pet-friendly, but that has certainly had its problems. I've got a chapter devoted to the question of allowing pets or not. More on that soon.

Amenities That Will Help Sell Your Guests on Your Property

Wi-Fi (the faster, the better)—Thanks to COVID and other world events, more and more people are traveling while working and they require top-of-the-line Wi-Fi. Technology is always changing, so do your own research on this and get the best that you can afford. It will pay for itself in the long run.

Fireplace—I understand this isn't always possible. In our Airstream it certainly isn't, but in Cottage West, we were concerned enough about the integrity of the chimney, that we ended up placing an electric fireplace unit into the space. It glows, it gives off heat, and some level of atmosphere, but it isn't a logs-crackling-in-the-fireplace kind of experience. That said, people enjoy it and use it.

Workout equipment (even a yoga mat)—In Cottage West, there is an enclosed back porch that is perfect for sipping coffee or practicing yoga, so I included two mats. I did the same with the Airstream, placing the yoga mats in a cabinet on the spacious outside deck. This has worked well, and

I've had multiple compliments over the years. I got the idea from Gimpy's, this adorable, colorful place I stayed at outside of Franklin, Tennessee. I was attending a conference there, and every morning, I sat out on the enclosed screen porch and practiced yoga. It was an excellent start to my day. Using workout equipment, or even something as simple as a yoga mat, can increase the production of serotonin, a "feel-good" chemical in our bodies. And this can lead to excellent reviews. Trust me on this!

Coffee maker/pour over/French press—Whether you provide a coffee maker, ceramic pour-over, or French press, add a few tea bags on the side as well. I caution against Keurig coffee pods. Not only are they poor quality, but they are expensive and wasteful. Many hosts complain guests will steal any excess K-cups. I stock ground coffee and fill up a jar and set it there on the coffee station. I provide a French press, along with instructions, and a ceramic pour-over, there in my Cottage West rental. In over three years, I have had only one guest complain *I didn't have a Keurig. The weird thing? They traveled with decaf K-cups, but didn't bother trying to open them and use them with the ceramic pour over, which would have worked just fine.*

Desk or work station—As mentioned above with Wi-Fi, the amount of people traveling (and working) is increasing exponentially, so it pays to have a workspace or desk if you have the room for it. The Tree of Life entry table I created for Cottage West (picture below) is quite spacious and I have had several traveling workers comment on it favorably.

Iron and ironing board—I don't own a single item of clothing that requires ironing. That said, providing an iron and ironing board can be a lifesaver for a traveler who needs to press a dress shirt. Steamers are also a nice touch.

Nightstands and reading lamps—Nightstands or equivalent furniture on each side of a bed, along with small reading lamps (bonus points if you can find them with USB chargers and electrical outlets) are essential. Guests love having multiple options. Having just one overhead light isn't enough.

Luggage racks—Simple, metal with fabric straps, folding luggage racks are the way to go. Squirrel them away in a closet, one for every bedroom.

<u>Dressers</u>—Even if your STRs have luggage racks, closets, and more—add a dresser to each bedroom. You never know when you will have a long-term guest, or even a guest who is staying a few days, who will want one.

<u>Swimming pool and/or hot tub</u>—These are huge draws for guests, but they do come with a need for maintenance, higher electricity and water bills, and other issues.

<u>Heat and air conditioning</u>—It's pretty standard, but it needs to be said. Unless you live in an area that is consistently at a year-round temperature of 70 degrees Fahrenheit, you will probably need heat and A/C. Central heat and A/C are the norm, so if you only have window units or space heaters, disclose that in the listing so guests know what to expect and don't end up giving a poor review because they didn't get what they expected.

<u>Television with cable/streaming services provided</u>—Guests expect some kind of basic entertainment package. With so many choices, you don't have to have standard cable any longer. We provide Netflix, Hulu, Curiosity Stream, and Amazon Prime to our guests, along with a digital receiver that allows guests to watch all the local stations.

A note next to each TV requesting that guests *not* sign out of the provided account and go into their own will avoid trouble down the road. We once received a less-than-stellar review after a previous guest had logged out of Netflix, and the most recent guest didn't know the login (never provide that password; just make sure it stays logged in) and assumed we had misled them in the listing description. Also, if you are close to your STR like we are, and share the login, you may wish to create a separate account for your guests. Otherwise, they change/mess with one of your own logins. The Airstream does not have a TV, so we simply made a Cottage West user account on Netflix and Hulu and Amazon for our guests, and that has worked out well.

<u>Toiletries (including good toilet paper)</u>—I will have a complete list later in the book, but just start thinking about what *you* would need/use in your home, and consider supplying that for your guests. You want them to feel at home, so how can you make that happen? Toiletries include cotton balls,

mouthwash, toothpaste, individually wrapped toothbrushes, ear plugs, analgesics, and so much more. And for goodness' sake, get the decent toilet paper! Cheap is as cheap does.

<u>Blankets, throws, sheet sets, and extra pillows</u>—I make sure there are at least four pillows on each bed, plus another two in the closet for each bedroom. Blankets, you can never have enough of. Same with throws. Again, you will get a specific list later in the book, but plan on these things.

Is an STR legal in your area?

Thanks to some poor actors, the legalities of operating an STR in your particular area are of particular concern. And they vary widely.

Trust me, you do not want to assume they are legal and find out later that your municipality banned them. In the summer of 2020, after skimming through the city codes in a small town to the south of Kansas City, I couldn't find anything that showed that short-term rentals weren't allowed. I sank $9,000 into fixes, new fixtures, improvements, and furnishings on our three-bedroom, two-bath house in Belton that had been a long-term rental. Six weeks after opening for business, I received a letter from the City of Belton informing me that STRs were prohibited and there would be no exemptions or workarounds.

I can still remember the guy from Codes telling me, "Ma'am, you are operating a hotel in a residential zoned area."

Oh, was I ever hot at the thought that he was calling my STR a *hotel*. A *hotel*? I was providing something far better than a *hotel*.

In the end, it was a far better scenario to continue to return to a long-term rental (LTR) because of the location of that property, which was 22 miles away. I prefer to be close to my STRs, *very close*, which is why they are all within view of my house. It also dissuades guests from throwing parties when they read my house is "right next door." I don't explain that "right next door" is actually at the far end of a 150'+ feet of garden space.

It was a hell of a lesson, one that I hope you do not repeat. Take my word for it, find out the scoop on codes and running an STR *before* you sink thousands of dollars into it.

I suggest calling the city or town hall and asking to speak to someone with the codes division; they should be able to answer your questions.

And it isn't a simple yes or no answer. In Kansas City, they have passed special legislation for short-term rentals. Depending on whether you are sharing your house or using a separate property (house, apartment, tiny house, etc.), there are different licenses and fees and qualifying hoops to jump through.

There is no searchable database of what a particular town might do. If you live in one of the bigger cities, it will be far easier to find out the exact requirements of operating your STR than it can be for small towns here in Missouri.

Do yourself a favor and find out what those qualifications are and adhere to them. Nothing spells catastrophe like a rollicking STR business that is suddenly under scrutiny (or a cease and desist) by the powers that be.

Is Everything in Working Order?

This assumes you have a property ready to go. But if you do, then you want to make sure everything is in working order. Do you have a squeaky door? Fix it. Leaking faucet? Fix it. A broken window? Replace the glass. And on and on.

Remember, we are still in the planning stages of creating your STR. Read on to learn more about themes and décor.

Themes and Décor

———

C hoosing a theme is a personal choice, but it is one you need to make. If you have a well-defined vision of how your property should look, then jump into it and make it happen. If not, consider one of the following options:

Minimalist

When choosing a minimalist look, "less is more" definitely applies. This means few knickknacks, muted colors, clean lines, and timeless well-made furniture and art.

Formal

If you love the look of elegant hotels or properly decorated public buildings such as the White House, then you are likely drawn to a formal style of decorating. Formal style includes matching pairs of furniture, elaborate window coverings, and antiques. These are doable, even in a short-term rental. A formal style will draw a specific clientele, so the surrounding neighborhood and building exteriors must match. Guests will also expect a higher price point.

Boho Chic

With a cozy atmosphere, layered eclecticism, and a lived-in feel, boho chic will provide a welcoming vibe to a traveler who loves books and art and... macrame? But seriously, I love boho chic. It has a great welcoming feel for guests. Your guests most likely be relaxed, fun-loving, and eclectic.

Casual

Also known as California Casual, it centers on neutral, soft colors on furniture and walls, furnishings that are inviting and comfortable, and it is related to the boho chic style.

Eclectic

Eclectic means a mix of textures, time periods, styles, trends and colors. It can be a lot, but I will admit that I absolutely love the style.

These are just a few of the basic decorating styles that come to mind. I would consider Cottage West to be a mix between eclectic and casual. There are also more thematic choices you can make.

Do you want to provide a stunningly *unique* STR experience? Consider some of the following listings that are out there on Airbnb and VRBO...

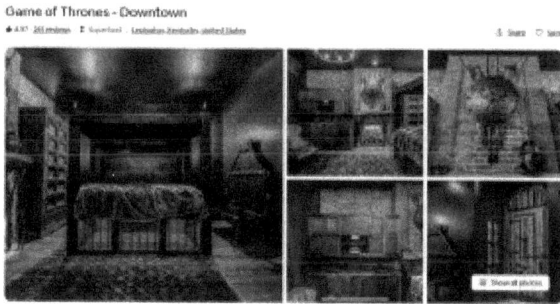

Game of Thrones - Downtown

Game of Thrones—Where you can be the lord or lady of a palatial chamber with a fur-covered bed and... mini dungeon?!

Link: https://www.airbnb.com/rooms/38573040

BACK to the 80s @ The McFly + Video Games & Cereal

The McFly-Back to the 80s—Which promises to make you feel like a kid in the 80s, complete with Ninja Turtles arcade and Nintendo.

Link: https://www.airbnb.com/rooms/26818996

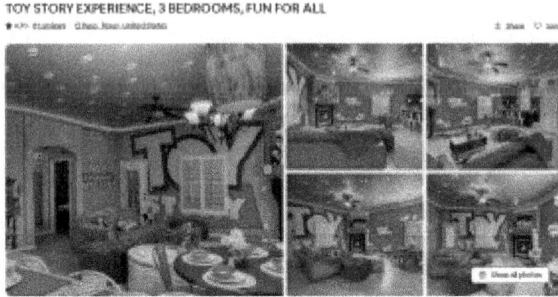

TOY STORY EXPERIENCE, 3 BEDROOMS, FUN FOR ALL

Toy Story Experience—If you love the movies, and your kids, this themed experience looks out of this world.

Link: https://www.airbnb.com/rooms/45942956

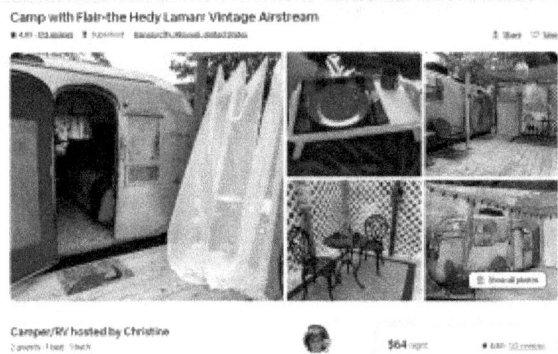

Camp with Flair-the Hedy Lamarr Vintage Airstream

Camper/RV hosted by Christine

Camp with Flair at the Hedy Lamarr—A unique and charming stay was forefront in my mind when I was preparing the Hedy Lamarr Airstream, our second STR, which was built in 1956. I wanted to pay homage to its history and kept the original cabinetry while adding a pinup girl motif. I also chose to *not* put a television inside of it. My one nod to the modern age was a vintage-look CD player and radio. I purchased the Best Hits of the 1950s in CDs to give folks a vintage vibe.

Link: https://airbnb.com/h/thehedylamarr

We will do something similar to our latest acquisition, a 1969 Holiday Rambler that I'm calling Proud Mary and decorating in fabrics and furnishings evocative of the late '60s, early '70s. I was a child of the 70s and I am here to tell you, in all honesty, I never, ever thought I would voluntarily return to that era in décor!

Remember, you will not hit the mark with every guest, you just aren't. Instead, imagine the guest you hope to attract. They are out there; I guarantee you! You just need to choose a theme or style and follow it. The guests who are interested will find you, especially if you offer a listing with plenty of pictures that show what you have chosen. We will talk more later about the photos that are important. For now, take a few notes, perhaps even suss out what furniture you have (or need to get) in order to create your own perfect STR theme or décor style.

Do your research, take your time. If themes and styles seem too much, know that it is perfectly acceptable to have a simple, straightforward STR. There are plenty of people who want a no-frills experience. You can wow them in other areas such as amenities or price. More on that soon.

Pets? Yes or No?

———

Will you allow pets in your short-term rental? A recent poll showed that over 67% of American households have pets. It should come as no surprise that more people are traveling with their pets and are actively looking for pet-friendly destinations.

Full disclosure here (if I haven't already let it slip), I am pet-friendly in our STRs. This has not come without its troubles, but I feel the benefits have outweighed the problems. That said, let's talk about the pros and cons of accepting pets into your short-term rental.

Pros

- You have the potential for more bookings by marketing your property to a wider audience

- You can increase your nightly rate (or include a pet fee), as pet owners will pay extra for the opportunity to stay with their pets.

- You have a competitive advantage over other properties that don't allow pets.

Cons

- Pets can cause damage and more wear and tear.

- Dogs, in particular, can be loud and disturb your neighbors.

- Most pets shed and this can cause an increase in mess and/or cleaning time/costs.

- It is possible for guests' pets to bring flea and tick infestations into your short-term rental.

- Some individuals (guests and hosts alike) are allergic to pet dander.

Let's discuss this for a moment. After three years of experience with allowing pets in our short-term rentals, I am still pet-friendly, but I have some advice and experience to share on the subject.

Potentially higher nightly income—I've listed the pros and the cons above, but I recommend allowing pets. This is one of those things that sets us apart from a standard hotel. And while hotels are beginning to accept animals, it is far less available than pet owners would like. Pet owners will be thankful you are pet-friendly, and there will be plenty of them who are just relieved they don't have to sneak them in. Because yes, that happens. A lot.

Allowing pets can also allow you to charge a nightly fee slightly higher than others in your area. It may seem like a conundrum, but a guest traveling with pets will often be willing to pay more for a place that allows pets than one that doesn't, and they will still balk at paying a pet fee.

Pet fees—There are pros and cons to charging a pet fee. For one, hosting platforms such as Airbnb only have a flat fee for pets. If you were to ask for $25, that would cover all the pets, whether there was one or four (or more). Some guests will do anything it takes to save a buck, and that includes misrepresenting how many pets they have, or disclosing if they have one with them at all. As I suggested above, I would simply suggest raising your nightly fee slightly higher instead. The other reason I don't charge pet fees is that some platforms (okay, Airbnb) do not honor damage claims on pets under their AirCover policy. If they see there is a pet, and you have pet-specific damage, you will not be compensated and you might not get any money from the guest either. They can simply ignore your request with no real repercussions (other than a negative review, which I have left).

Damage will happen. Plan accordingly—Let me start this off by saying that if you have wall-to-wall carpet in your STR, I actually advise that you *do not* allow pets. We went to area rugs over laminate, hardwood, vinyl and tile around 20 years ago. As a lifelong pet owner, I've found wall-to-wall carpeting especially disgusting just in the normal course of living. Factor in pets and children, and wall to wall carpeting is a nightmare. An area rug can be cleaned or replaced for a relatively inexpensive investment, but regular carpeting cannot be.

Imagine, for a moment, that you are a dog (or a cat). You can smell everything, every creature that has stayed in this strange place you are currently staying in. No matter how well-behaved your owners think you are, the likelihood is, with smelling all of those smells, even the best dog will crack. The place is unfamiliar, and look, right here, some dog peed. You can smell it.

Most pet owners will do their absolute level best to anticipate their pets' needs and avoid messes and clean them up when they happen. A smaller percentage will not.

Over time, I have found that even area rugs are not something that belongs in our STR properties, and they are being slowly phased out as stains and other mishaps occur. We will be left with hardwood and tile floors that are easily cleaned and maintained. I also suggest stocking an enzyme cleaner that can be added to the mop water. This will help remove the smell of the other animals and their accidents. I've listed it in the Cleaning Supplies list which is available for download on my author website:

https://www.christineshuck.com/str-success-resources.

And if you have damage that has resulted from a pet, I recommend the following course of action:

- Reach out to the guest. Something to the effect of, "Hi Susan, my cleaners noticed that there was a hole in the couch cushion that wasn't there at the last turn-over." Wait for a response. They will either own up to it or not. If they do, typically they will offer to pay or ask you what you want from them. Then you can send them a damage request via the online platform. Some platforms have built-in damage deposits as part of the reservation and it simply goes against that and paid out to you.

- Contact the online platform. I typically avoid using any verbiage that indicates it might have been a pet that did this damage since some platforms (Airbnb) do not honor pet damages at the time of this writing as part of their host insurance. I had this recently happen to two rugs. The guest was unresponsive to my request, so I escalated to Airbnb and wrote, "They damaged two rugs during the guest's stay. One may have had something spilled on it, as it was washed, and the other had two holes worn in it. Perhaps from a chair leg?" Within 24 hours, they issued payment for the replacement costs of both rugs. I chose not to purchase replacement rugs, since the hardwood floors are easier to maintain.

Service animals and emotional support animals

Whether you choose to accept pets, please remember that service animals are legally allowed in *all* United States housing per the Americans with Disabilities Act. There is a significant amount of confusion on what a service animal is, and how it is differentiated from an emotional support animal, so I want to address that clearly and concisely so that you have zero confusion on it.

As defined on ADA.gov (link listed below) on ADA.gov, a service animal is defined as *"dogs that are individually trained to work or perform tasks for people with disabilities."* The ADA clarifies what that means. *"Examples of such work or tasks include guiding people who are blind, alerting people who are deaf, pulling a wheelchair, alerting and protecting a person who is having a seizure, reminding a person with mental illness to take prescribed medications, calming a person with Post Traumatic Stress Disorder (PTSD) during an anxiety attack, or performing other duties. Service animals are working animals, not pets."*

As a working animal, you *cannot* request an additional deposit or pet fee from your guest. You also *cannot,* by law, deny a reservation request from a potential guest solely because of a no pet policy you may have in place. That's for a service animal, *not* an emotional support animal.

"Okay, great," you might think, "Then what the heck are emotional support animals?"

An emotional support animal is an animal companion that offers some type of benefit to an individual with some form of disability. The animal should provide companionship and support that will help ease at least the emotional aspect of the disability. Also, dogs are the most common type of emotional support animal, but cats are quite common as well. Other types of animals, such as miniature horses, can also serve as ESAs. Per the ADA, *"Dogs whose sole function is to provide comfort or emotional support do not qualify as service animals under the ADA."*

Link: https://www.ada.gov/service_animals_2010.htm

Emotional support animals do not qualify as a service animal and therefore, as a host, you are not required under law to accept them.

I have copied the following directly from the ADA website and is very important for you to read and understand when dealing with a potential or current guest who has an ADA-compliant service animal. I've also highlighted the particularly host-applicable points:

- When it is not obvious what service an animal provides, only limited inquiries are allowed. Staff may ask two questions: (1) is the dog a service animal required because of a disability, and (2) What work or task has the dog been trained to perform? Staff cannot ask about the person's disability, require medical documentation, require a special identification card or training documentation for the dog, or ask that the dog show its ability to perform the work or task.

- Allergies and fear of dogs are not valid reasons for denying access or refusing service to people using service animals. When a person who is allergic to dog dander and a person who uses a service animal must spend time in the same room or facility, for example, in a school classroom or at a homeless shelter, they both should be accommodated by assigning them, if possible, to

61

different locations within the room or different rooms in the facility.

• A person with a disability cannot be asked to remove his service animal from the premises unless: (1) the dog is out of control and the handler does not take effective action to control it or (2) the dog is not housebroken. When there is a legitimate reason to ask that a service animal be removed, staff must offer the person with the disability the opportunity to obtain goods or services without the animal's presence.

• Establishments that sell or prepare food must allow service animals in public areas even if state or local health codes prohibit animals on the premises.

• People with disabilities who use service animals cannot be isolated from other patrons, treated less favorably than other patrons, or charged fees that are not charged to other patrons without animals. In addition, if a business requires a deposit or fee to be paid by patrons with pets, it must waive the charge for service animals.

• If a business such as a hotel normally charges guests for damage that they cause, a customer with a disability may also be charged for damage caused by himself or his service animal.

• Staff are not required to provide care for or supervision of a service animal.

Keep in mind if/when dealing with customer service of an online booking program that you may have to educate them as to the ADA website and laws quoted. This is definitely an important section to bookmark if you have future dealings on the subject.

What to Stock

After all that, if you choose to allow pets, I recommend you stock the following in your STR to help your pet owners out:

- A water and food bowl

- Puppy pads

- Enzyme/deodorizing spray

- Chew toys/cat toys

- Mat for placing bowls on for floor

- Wire kennel

Stocking these items, most of which you can find for next to nothing at a local dollar store, can mean the world for pet owners. The wire kennel can also mean the difference between an owner letting their pets roam free and damaging your home. I've had many guests comment that in providing the kennel, I had saved them the trouble of having to unpack theirs and haul it inside.

Whew! That was a lot of information! In summary, accepting pets in your STR can mean potentially more income. It can also come with drawbacks. And when dealing with a potential service animal, it can come with plenty of rules and regulations.

Moving on, we will now talk about children, and where you want to be on the welcome scale with having them in your short-term rental!

Children? Yes or No?

I ask this partially tongue in cheek, but it is actually something to discuss. Do you have a property that is *not* conducive to children? Maybe you are concerned about a pool on the property that has no fence. Hey, maybe you don't like children. No judgment here. Sometimes, even as a parent, I can completely relate to the following message left by a guest at Cottage West on the refrigerator, which holds some fun random word magnets...

Hey, it gave me a good laugh!

Per the terms of service of most hosting platforms, specifically VRBO and Airbnb, you *cannot* prevent guests with children from booking your STR. There are those pesky rules in place about housing discrimination, etc.

I recommend that you either make your STR child-friendly or state clearly in the listing description the reasons it is not appropriate for children and then let the guests make their own determination.

- This STR is in the middle of a nudist colony (this won't deter all guests, by the way)

- Our pool/hot tub is unsecured by a safety fence

- The open floor plan does not allow for safety gates for toddlers and infants to be put in place

And so on.

Just as I am all for allowing pets, I also recommend allowing children—and not just because I'm a pet owner and mother of four kids. It makes financial sense. Making your STR available to as many people as possible equals more bookings and more money. Plain and simple.

How to Make Your STR Kid-Friendly

While it is impossible to anticipate age or interest, I recommend having the following in your STR:

- High chair (freestanding or one that hooks onto a table)

- Playpen

- Kids' dishes

- Assortment of books (I provide everything from board books to teen and adult reading-level books)

- Kids games/activity books

- Covers for outlets

- Video games

- Rooms specifically decorated and furnished for children

- Game rooms with air hockey, foosball and more

The first three are a must if you want to be even the least bit family-friendly. The rest will push your STR into the family favorite range and straight over the top.

Keep in mind, however, that all people, not just kids, can be hard on electronics. Think about that before investing in, and turning your guests loose on, expensive video games and more. Or charge a price that allows for regular maintenance, repair, and/or replacement of such devices.

Rental Insurance

———

L et's talk insurance, folks.

I'll be honest. When I got to this chapter, I wasn't sure how to go about it. Until the writing of this book, I had utilized standard landlord insurance. If something happened, only the structure itself would be covered, not the interior furnishings, décor, or appliances. Why had I done this? Well, it was cheaper. Quite a bit cheaper. As in half as much. My insurance premium on Cottage West, my two-bedroom, one-bath house, was just $767 per year last year. And I will say that I've operated Cottage West for three years with little trouble or expense. We've had our adventures, to be sure. We've dealt with:

- Locals who smoked marijuana inside of the property, shot off a gun outside (it was New Year's), and then tried to get a refund by claiming one of them had woken up with a rash and they had seen a mouse.

- Another local who moved in overnight on a one-night stay. It looked as if they brought the entire contents of their apartment with them, including televisions, décor, and more.

- A guest whose dog ate two rugs during the two-day stay.

- A male prostitute who tried to break into the basement (likely to steal the copper). He succeeded only in breaking two new knives.

- A termite infestation.

- Multiple rodent infestations, one of which ended in a full refund being issued to the guests by Airbnb after their stay (they refused to leave their three-night stay even for a partial refund, and then requested a refund in full directly from Airbnb, who granted it).

But as stressful as these events were, they were easily overcome. I've been lucky. I've never gotten bed bugs, for one. After I did the research on that, and the subsequent costs, the saying "penny wise and pound foolish" came to mind. Let's just say that when it came to this chapter, my research was eye-opening. One incident of bed bugs and you will be out around $750 - $1,800 for the treatment alone. And that's not counting lost income because of having to refund a guest who finds the bedbugs, or needing to cancel an incoming guest before they can eradicate the bedbugs. Recent advancements in pest control have meant that heat treatment (which was often twice as costly as the figures above, and shut down the property being treated for at least 24 hours), has now been replaced by a quicker chemical treatment. Bed bugs are a nightmare I have never had to deal with and hope never to have to. However, they were an important factor when I took a deep look at insurance companies that specialized in short-term rental insurance.

After researching the different issues that can come up with a short-term rental and running down a list of the differences, I am convinced that an insurance intended specifically for short-term rentals is a *must* for hosts who are operating a stand-alone property (i.e., not a property you live at or one that you rent through rental arbitrage) and here is why:

Common short-term rental coverages include:

- Loss of income
- Excess use of utilities
- Infestation (bedbugs, termites, ants, cockroaches, etc.)
- Liquor liability
- Identity theft

Here is a screenshot of the coverage quote from Proper for Cottage West:

Limits of Insurance	
Commercial General Liability Coverage	**Limit**
Each Occurrence*	$1,000,000
General Aggregate*	$2,000,000
Personal & Advertising Injury with Invasion of Privacy	$1,000,000
Liquor Liability	$1,000,000
Animal/Pet Liability	$1,000,000
Communicable Disease	$1,000,000
Assault & Battery with Sexual Molestation	$1,000,000
Amenities On & Off Premises (Hot Tubs, Pools, Docks, Bicycles, Kayaks, etc.)	$1,000,000
*Higher Liability Limits Available	
Included Policy Coverage Enhancements	**Limit**
Backup of Sewers & Drains	$25,000
Collapse Including Sinkhole, Weight of Ice, Snow, People	Included
Debris Removal	Included
Unscheduled Structures	$10,000
Optional Policy Coverage Enhancements	**Limit**
Ordinance or Law - Undamaged Portion of Building	Building(s) Limit
Ordinance or Law - Increased Cost of Construction	$50,000
Bed Bug Extermination & Business Revenue - No Deductible	$15,000
Squatters & Eviction Expenses Plus Business Revenue - No Deductible	$15,000
Business Income Coverage	**Limit**
Total for all Locations	$10,000
Time Limitation	Unlimited
Actual Loss of Gross Revenue	Included
Deductibles (other deductible options may be available)	**Deductible**
Property Deductible	$1,000
Liability Deductible	$0
Wind Deductible	$1,000

Frankly, I was dazzled by this coverage. Pretty much everything listed under the Commercial General Liability Coverage had me interested in learning more, and when I saw the Optional Policy Coverage Enhancements (namely "Bed Bug Extermination & Business Revenue-No Deductible"), they sold me. This wasn't just good insurance; this was *great* insurance. The total came in at $1,850 per year for coverage. Yes, it was more than twice what I was paying for landlord's insurance, but one incidence of bedbugs and the annual premium would pay for itself.

I didn't want to stop there, however, so I reached out to a couple more STR insurers for more quotes. Lemonade, which came highly recommended, was unable or unwilling to provide a quote. I am unsure why, but I suspect it is the age of my property. Cottage West was built in 1920, and while we have renovated it from top to bottom with just about everything—new roof, windows, insulation, drywall, wiring, plumbing and HVAC—the age of the property seemed to be an issue. When I reached out to Farmer's, they insisted on bundling the homeowner's insurance quote (it did not give an option specifically for STR insurance) with auto or life insurance when I tried online. Without bundling, I was faced with calling the company for a quote rather than requesting it online. I filled out another extensive online quote request with CBIZ that is considered "best for vacation homes" by Investopedia and received a staggering quote of $5,650 per year. Um, no thank you. Finally, I received a call from Foremost Insurance, which had initially told me they could not provide me with a quote online. After some informational questions, I received a quote of $3,336—3,501 annual premium, depending on whether I chose a $1,000 deductible or a $500 deductible. Also, I learned that Foremost does not provide bed bug coverage.

I chose Proper for our coverage. They were thorough, straightforward, and knowledgeable. The process was straightforward as well. Their prices seemed reasonable (when compared to the other STR-specific quotes) and their overall coverage was just what we were looking for. They also impressed me with the reviews of them on the Better Business Bureau that showed their customer service was excellent and their claim payouts were relatively trouble-free. That said, it is vital that you take the time to shop around. Your experience might not be my experience, and finding the right insurance is a vital part of starting your STR journey off on the right foot.

Here are some specific areas to look at if you currently have a standard homeowner's or landlord's insurance policy:

A few STR-specific coverages to think about

- Do I have at least $300,000 in liability coverage limits? *Note: check your own local area's requirements. In my city, a minimum of $300k in liability is required for our STR license.*

- Does my liability extend to off-premises in the event a guest is injured off my premises?

- Does my liability coverage extend to my amenities such as swimming pools, hot tubs, bicycles, and more? (As needed, of course)

- Do I have liquor liability coverage in the event I get pulled into a lawsuit surrounding alcohol use of a short-term rental guest?

- Does my coverage exclude assault and battery or invasion of privacy?

- Does my property insurance have limits on the damage caused by a guest?

- Do I carry bed bug coverage for both property and liability?

- In the event of an insurance claim, does my coverage include lost business income, and is there a time limit?

- Have I read actual STR insurance claims reviews regarding the insurance provider?

Here is the list of companies I found who *claim* to specialize in short-term rental insurance. There are undoubtedly more out there, so please do your own research and talk to other hosts about their own personal experiences. The major companies specializing in short-term rental insurance include, but are not limited to:

- Allstate

- American Family

- American Modern

- CBIZ

- Farmer's

- Lemonade

- Nationwide

- Proper

Next up? Anticipating costs for your STR.

Anticipating Costs

———

Costs for startup can vary wildly based on what you have readily available and what you will need to buy for your space. Are you going for a high-end look? Boho thrift? Does the space already have the appliances (refrigerator, stove, washer/dryer, etc)? Has this space served as a long-term rental in the past?

I can, however, give you some basic costs, based on my shopping choices. Again, keep in mind that your costs will vary depending on the space provided and what you currently have on hand. In my case, I was furnishing an entire house. In another, an RV with built-ins, no need for furniture, only one bed, and extremely limited storage space. At present, my two STRs are:

- Cottage West—a two-bedroom, one-bath home with access to a large, shared yard

- The Hedy Lamarr Airstream—a unique two-guest-max stay in our large yard

Your rental property will vary from mine. The various factors involved-location, prices (including recent inflation), amenities, and purpose (why guests choose your property) all drive the startup costs and, later, the cost to maintain that property. Despite this, we can cobble together some numbers that will help you anticipate your initial outlay.

As an example, I'm going to use Cottage West, our first STR property. I'm also going to assume that there are no major renovations necessary and that the property is ready to be furnished, decorated, and filled with supplies.

Cottage West Startup Costs

Here is a table that gives you a basic idea of what I would recommend to someone who is rolling out their first property (I used Cottage West as the model):

Mortgage and Utilities:	
Mortgage x 3 months	$1,515.00
Utilities x 3 months	$825.00
Internet, streaming svcs x 3 months (Google ($70), Netflix ($19.99), Hulu($6.99)	$290.94
Furniture and décor:	
Furniture (mix of used pieces & mattresses)	$2,000.00
Décor	$500.00
Pillows, bed linens, bath linens, kitchen linens	$800.00
Kitchen Appliances (assuming major appliances are already there)	$200.00
Cookware, dishes, glassware, utensils	$750.00
Cleaning Supplies, paper towels, etc	$200.00
Total Anticipated Startup Costs:	**$7,080.94**

I have added a Startup Costs worksheet to the Complete STR Financial Tracking spreadsheet. You can download that here at my author website: https://christineshuck.com/str-success-resources. It is easy to edit. You can create your own specific list of expenses that way.

Why three months? —You may have noticed above that I figured on three months' worth of mortgage/rent, utilities, and internet/streaming services. It shouldn't take you that long to see a profit. Honestly, I would be surprised if it did. But it is important to have funds to fall back on in case you have a rocky start. By having a three-month cushion, you know that if you somehow forgot to buy extra blankets, or your refrigerator goes kaput, you have something to fall back on. I plan as conservatively as possible and squirrel extra funds away wherever possible. Doing so is a step towards protecting yourself against the unexpected. And speaking of the unexpected...

Plan for the unexpected—Unless you are using the rental arbitrage model, where you simply sub-lease an apartment or house, you need to plan for maintenance and repairs to the building besides the furnishings within. Often these are simply standard wear-and-tear repairs, and insurance does not cover many of these things. And even if you *are* doing rental arbitrage and don't own the building, if a leak develops and ruins a couch or bed, you will still need to buy a new couch or bed, even if that amount is later refunded under your renter's insurance. And no matter what, during the time of repair, you may experience a loss of rental income. This is why it is so important to plan for the unexpected.

I established a separate savings account I call my *Rental Slush* fund. From every rental deposit I receive, I place 15% of that income directly into an interest-bearing savings account.

It serves two purposes: it sets aside monies for any income taxes that remain after expenses are considered, and it helps cover me in case I need any major repairs or suffer any loss of income. I made this very easy with Airbnb payouts, where you can set up multiple bank accounts and specify a percentage of earnings to be deposited in each. The other booking platforms don't seem to have this option yet, but I expect that will change soon.

This automatic savings helps smooth the bumps out of my monthly operating costs. For example, we have a 100-plus-year-old cottonwood tree behind Cottage West. Soon after opening for business, I was over one evening and noticed that one bedroom seemed rather dimly lit. When I looked out of the window, I realized it was also a little more *green* than I remembered it—a massive limb had fallen, gouging a hole in the back porch roof!

With a $1,000 deductible, the $200 patch to the roof wasn't worth an increased annual premium, so we paid for it out of pocket. Thanks to the *Rental Slush* fund, it wasn't a painful pinch in the pocket, but simply one that had already been anticipated.

Rental Slush can also serve a third purpose: that of providing a source of funds to draw upon in the slow season, meaning you can set your STR income at a certain level and draw on it much the same as you would a paycheck. I do this. With my current two STRs and one long-term rental, I expect to earn a net income of $3,000 per month, year-round. Note: I also set aside $1,500 per month into a renovations fund for future projects and funnel any additional net income amounts beyond that $3,000 into a renovations fund. If you aren't planning any additional short-term rentals, then you obviously wouldn't need a renovations fund and could add that income directly to your earnings. I deposit that $3,000 into a personal checking account at the first of every month. In the middle of winter, our slow season, I've seen two months in the past year where my net income was below $3,000. Thanks to the *Rental Slush* fund, our monthly income remained unaffected, even in our slowest season. And in the busy season, we often see up to $1,400 in excess funds that we can put into slush or a separate account tagged, especially for renovations of future projects!

Definitely consider downloading the *Complete STR Financial Tracking* spreadsheet. The spreadsheets will help you identify and add your various expenses so that you can be prepared for the financial outlay necessary. You can visit my author website to see all documents available for free download at: **https://www.christineshuck.com/str-success-resources**. I have also prepared some rather exhaustive shopping lists which you will also find there on the Resources page of my website.

What Do YOU Expect from Your Guests?

B efore we get too deep into putting your STR in action, I would like to stop for a moment and talk about your expectations of a potential guest. I mention this because the original concept of Airbnb, complete with its air mattresses on the floor, home-sharing-platform, has changed. And it has changed drastically.

As I was writing this book, the news stories have changed from "out of control, unregulated party houses," to "Airbnb hosts charge exorbitant cleaning fees AND give guests chores lists."

The Wall Street Journal recently posted an article, *Welcome to Your Airbnb, the Cleaning Fees Are $143 and You'll Still Have to Wash the Linens.* What followed was a scathing assessment of the high fees and long chores lists that are scaring away guests from using Airbnb and other online booking platforms.

As I mentioned in the first chapter, we can do better. And we must do better if we want short-term rentals to survive and *thrive.* We provide a vital middle-ground between hotels and bed and breakfasts. We offer autonomy like hotels, and less personal service as bed and breakfasts, but with the ability to do more (cook in a kitchen, play lawn darts on a back lawn, or watch Netflix and Hulu).

As for *my* expectations of guests, they are relatively simple:

- Have a basic level of respect for the space (i.e., don't trash it)

- Be a responsible pet owner (don't let them pee and poop inside or eat my furniture and if they do, be an adult about it and take responsibility)

- Be a responsible parent (don't let your kids run feral and draw on the walls or furniture)

- If you have time to do the dishes—great!

- No parties and no smoking indoors

That's basically it. There are no chores lists. No requests for trash to be taken out since the cleaner (usually me) is there same day of checkout to clean. I don't particularly even want them to strip the beds since I have a particular way of doing laundry and heaven forbid, they should start a load for me; my poor obsessive-compulsive self can barely stand it when they do!

You are an adult, and you can make your own choices on how you wish to run your STR business. That said, if you wish to be in business for a long time, cut out the chores list, pump up the hospitality, and let your guests relax. After all, that is a huge part of why they are there.

Part III: Creating the Perfect Space

———

Preparing the Space

———

O ne reason that Airbnb, VRBO, and other short-term rentals have taken off is because they differ vastly from hotels. And their differences make them unique.

Hotels provide ice, terrible coffee, and maybe a microwave and mini-fridge. They provide the same rooms, over and over. The same furniture, the same wallpaper, curtains, and bathrooms. They thrive on sameness and a spartan decorative style.

We can do more, be more, and provide more—easily, and often for a much more affordable price.

I've made a few lists. They can all be downloaded here at my author website: https://www.christineshuck.com/str-success-resources

These are all items I provide in my properties. I have had *so many* positive comments on these thoughtful touches that I can tell you the money I have spent has been worth every penny. In most cases, they are inexpensive, but they definitely make an impression. When guests walk into one of my properties, they know they are in their home away from home.

Consider topping up these supplies between each guest, or schedule a regular supply level check-in. Nothing says "I've expected your arrival" like a completely full shampoo and conditioner dispenser, a row of toilet paper rolls, etc. It makes a difference between a guest feeling like they are a last-minute, rushed consideration or feeling that they have been planned for and their needs anticipated.

I have a question for you. How many times have you been traveling and forgot something? Maybe you forgot your charger to your phone? Or possibly noticed you have a sore throat after all that air travel and need a lozenge? Did the airport food give you indigestion? Have you forgotten to bring cotton swabs?

Having these things available means you don't have to find a store in the middle of a city or town you don't know your way around. It means being able to get comfort, relief, or stay in touch with friends without additional effort, sometimes when afflicted in the wee hours of the night. When you provide these to your guests, it also means a guest will be more likely to give you a 5-star review when they leave. Below, I'm going to go into the details of what preparing your space entails, room by room, but first, let's talk about guest access...

Guest access—I'll cut right to the chase. You want a keyless entry lock. It allows for guests to access the property without you having to meet them there, and it removes the problem of having keys lost by the guests. This is especially important if you are not local, as a lost key causes all kinds of havoc, not the least having to re-key the locks. Better to have a keyless entry lock, where the guest is issued their own unique code. Bonus points if you can find one that can be accessed remotely from a smartphone app, where you can add a new code or delete a compromised code from afar. There are a few out on the market that other hosts highly recommend. Consider the following brands: Yale-August, Schlage Encode, Kwikset Aura. We currently use the Ultraloq smart lock. It is Bluetooth capable and can be easily and quickly programmed. You can find it here:

https://amzn.to/3EzbNzR.

With guest access, make it as easy as possible, while remaining secure. Guests should be able to check themselves in without your presence. This is especially important in areas where guests are arriving at varying times of the day and night. Do you really want to be trying to coordinate your schedule to theirs? Give them the autonomy and ability to check themselves in.

Now, let's talk about what your short-term rental should have. We will take this room by room...

Living rooms—Think comfort, think style, and by all means, think welcoming! A living room should be comfortable, and roomy enough for multiple guests to enjoy the space without feeling cramped or uncomfortable. While bedrooms are extremely important, the common living spaces must also be welcoming and offer a variety of entertainment options for the guest.

Entertainment—Living rooms are often where a television is provided. The bedrooms are also a possibility, depending upon space constraints. In Cottage West, a two-bedroom, one bath bungalow, we chose to only have one television and locate it in the living room. The Roku flat-screen televisions are relatively affordable. You should be able to find one for under $400. A Roku can connect to Wi-Fi and you can connect an antenna to local digital channels. With it, I suggest providing at least two to three streaming services. We provide Netflix, Curiosity Stream and Amazon Prime Video. But don't stop at a television! Consider board games (standard checkers, chess, Monopoly or backgammon), card games, books that have crosswords, word searches, Sudoku, and more. As an author, it is especially important for me to have a mini library in each of my short-term rentals. Even the Hedy Lamarr Airstream has a mini library! Visit garage sales or used bookstores to find a variety of genres and interests. I have a note up that tells guests that if they like and want a book, take it, and either leave a book in its place or a tip for the book fairy. It's based on the honor system and most of the books I have in my STRs, I spent $2 or less on, and I frequently receive a $5 tip, or more. This more than covers any expenses. Guests enjoy having a wide range of entertainment offerings, so be sure to leave a few magazines around as well.

Rest/comfort/privacy—Living rooms are a great place for couches to double as beds. If you have the room, consider a couch that converts to a bed or is long enough to serve as a twin size bed. Our bungalow's living room is relatively small, but there was enough room for two couches strategically placed. One is firmer, while the other is rather squishy. They both work well for our guests' needs. Try to choose couches that are durable and well-made, pieces that won't be easily stained or damaged. Bonus points if you can remove the cushion covers and wash them in a pinch. Guests can be hard on furniture. If space allows, include armchairs, coffee tables and plenty of places for guests to set their drinks or food down. Be aware, guests might find a living room the perfect place to eat their meals rather than a dining room. That might not be *your* first choice, but you aren't their parents and crumbs on the couch will happen! Finally, consider blackout curtains for any windows, both for privacy and also comfort for those who fall asleep on the couches. This isn't an absolute must. It might not work at all for your property, especially if it means blocking a scenic view or if you have taller than average windows. So, take that advice with a grain of salt.

Work/desk space—If possible, include a work space into the design of your living room. In Cottage West, the living room doubles as the front entry to the house, and we installed a long entry table that does double duty as the welcome area and also as a workspace for those who are working while traveling. These spaces should have at least enough room for a laptop along with a decent chair and at least two free open outlets for anything that needs to be plugged in. A small desk lamp can also be very helpful. I include a notepad, spare pens, along with note cards and stationery in a drawer for my guests. I also stock a charger, with varying different cables, capable of charging whatever device a guest might have. This has been a lifesaver for many guests.

Décor—Don't forget the walls! Following your chosen theme, or even a basic travel theme as I have, add framed pictures, art and more to your walls to create a cozy, welcoming feel.

Kitchens—Kitchens put us a step above hotels and motels. Here is your chance to shine!

Coffee, tea, and water—Before you click BUY on that Keurig coffeemaker, let me offer some advice and suggest you do NOT have one. Keurig coffees are gross, watery versions of what coffee can and should taste like. As I mentioned before, they are overpriced and wasteful. Instead, consider a pour over ceramic that takes filters, or my favorite, a French press. Specifically, I use a durable stainless steel French Press and the ceramic pour over with filters and they continue to perform year after year. In over three years of operation, I have had one guest complain we didn't have a Keurig. The ironic part of this? They could have easily used the French press or ceramic pour-over by simply emptying their K-cup inside! I provide a medium-roast coffee, as well as a decaf version, and a mix of caffeinated and herbal tea varieties. I also recommend an electric water kettle. It heats water quickly and efficiently. I have labeled mine clearly so guests don't get confused and set it on the stovetop. Set up a little coffee/tea station if you have room for it. I try to keep shelf-stable creamer, sugar, and all four artificial/non-sugar sweeteners (saccharine, aspartame, stevia, and sucralose) available as well. Finally, you may wish to consider stocking purified water or a Britta water filter in the refrigerator. I've had a couple of guests who felt uncomfortable with the water or its taste and bought their own purified water. Personally, I like the taste of our water and I know it is safe (having tested it for impurities because of the age of our homes and the fact that we have young children who are especially sensitive to lead levels), but more and more I'm leaning toward providing a Britta pitcher in the refrigerator for our guests ease of mind.

Appliances—The standard appliances are a refrigerator, toaster, microwave, stove, and, as I mentioned above, an electric water kettle (optional, but highly recommended). If you know you will have longer stays, you definitely also want to have an oven for any of their baking needs. I prefer a toaster oven over a standard toaster since it has the added benefit of being able to bake smaller items (tater tots, small pizzas, etc.) and also everything from toast to bagels, which some toasters can't handle. A dishwasher is nice, but not 100% necessary unless you are providing an STR that is in the mid to higher price ranges. Check your competition in that area. We do not provide them in any of our STRs, but that is more a matter of space issues than anything else. If you have a dishwasher, you will want to make sure and stock the dish detergent tablets rather than a bottle of detergent. This helps prevent over-use of the soap. For those hosts who set out tablets, they give guests a few of them, to prevent theft. I would suggest setting out one tablet for each day of their stay.

Dishes, cookware and more—You should have enough dishes to feed the maximum number of guests your STR allows for. Same for silverware, although I would suggest possibly doubling that number. We provide twelve each of (big fork, small fork, big spoon, small spoon, and knife) and a set of six steak knives in Cottage West (which can hold six guests total). The dishes should be in good condition (no cracks, scratches, or chips). Consider stocking a set of children's dishes as well. I recently added this to our listing, and it has been received gratefully by parents traveling with little ones. It's also saved dishes from being broken! As far as cookware goes, I suggest non-stick for frying pans. Don't get the cheapest of the cheap, as they will be scratched up in no time. However, I also wouldn't advise high-end pieces as guests rarely realize that the high temps can damage them. A set of graduated in size pots is a good idea as well. Most guests will not expect extensive cookware, unless you bill your STR as having a gourmet kitchen, so be reasonable about this. Be sure to pick up a decent set of cooking utensils (suited for non-stick), and make sure you have included measuring spoons, cups, and a pair of kitchen shears.

I also include an assortment of inexpensive plastic baggies I purchase at a discount store—snack, sandwich, quart, and gallon sizes. For towels and dishcloths, I recommend dark colors and sturdy fabrics (cotton blends). Guests are hard on these items and after spending an inordinate amount of time trying to get stains out of the lighter pieces, I realized I was far better off with dark colors that didn't show the stains. Supply napkins and have a roll of paper towels available for guests to use. You will also want to stock hand soap, dish soap, a dish brush, a blue scrub sponge, and a green abrasive scrubber for guests to use should they wish to clean up after themselves. I also keep one or two extra kitchen trash bags below the sink and then put the rest in a supply closet.

I've created extensive, detailed lists which you can download for free from my author website: **https://www.christineshuck.com/ str-success-resources**. It's great to have these in the future as a reference for when you need to re-stock these items.

One piece of advice: don't be chintzy and cheap. Don't leave out a single roll of toilet paper or charge your guests for using an extra towel. Stock your properties well and provide your guests with abundance. Yes, there will be the occasional rarity of guest who blow through every additional towel and use toilet paper by the case. It's a rare thing, really it is. Most guests are reasonable, decent human beings who appreciate more than anything being treated like the adults that they are.

Bathrooms

I stayed in a fantastic STR outside of Franklin, Tennessee in 2019 while attending the TRIBE conference. I loved every single part of it, except for two things—the a/c unit that gave off a swampy smell that pervaded the entire unit and the thinnest toilet paper in the world. Despite these two things, I LOVED that place. I think I could have stayed there forever except I would have had to go out and buy some better toilet paper because that thin stuff just wasn't cutting it. They had stocked the bathroom with this absolutely heavenly scented shampoo and conditioner, but also the cheapest toilet paper they could find. It was quite odd.

In Part XI: Spreadsheets and Lists you will see a comprehensive list of what I believe every STR bathroom should contain. It is a long list and there aren't a ton of decisions to be made as there are in other parts of the house. In my detailed lists that are available for download, I have even included product links to make it easy for you to buy all the necessary supplies.

Bedrooms

Finally, we have arrived at the bedroom, one of the most important rooms in the house! Your guests, whether they stay one night or thirty, are looking for comfort, convenience, and a pleasant night's sleep. Here is how you will help them get it.

Bed—With a bed, there are a few decisions to make:

- What size bed

- What kind of frame

- Which mattress

- Linens and more

We are going to tackle those in order.

Size—Early on, I decided on queen-size beds, *not* king. Queen sheet sets are less expensive than king-size. Second, the queen beds are large enough to hold two adults or even up to three kids, and my rooms are on the smaller side. Third, king-size beds mean king-size pillowcases are included in the sheet set. I don't know about you, but I've never had king-size pillows, so the pillowcases either need to be altered (which I never get around to) or I have to buy separate (yet matching) standard pillowcases.

I have an exception to this rule. Cottage West, our first Airbnb, is a small, 900-square-foot bungalow with tiny rooms. In one room, we managed a queen, with a nightstand on either side, but the smaller bedroom simply couldn't fit the *length* of a queen-size bed (queens are 80 inches long, doubles are 75 inches long). We put in a full-size bed instead of a queen. We have had zero complaints about it so far.

I have seen hosts focus obsessively on king-size beds, often to the point of cramming one into a tiny bedroom that required one side of the bed to be pushed up against the wall. This is inconvenient for guests and cleaners alike. Guests don't want to climb over their partners to get off of the bed. My husband and I stayed in an Airbnb in London that was like that and it was a pain. When at all possible, make sure there is room on both sides of a bed for guests to access. Your cleaners will thank you as well.

And even more important than bed size is the mattress you choose. You need something that hovers between firm and squishy, and one that will last for as long as possible.

Frame—Pick a frame that won't creak and that can take some level of activity and use. Not to explain it in excruciating detail, but your guests will use the bed for far more than just sleeping in, so be sure that you don't have a cheap, easily broken frame!

Mattress—It is impossible to please everyone in this department. There are guests who want to sink into a mattress and others who want something firmer. The range of mattresses can vary extremely, so here are a few brand-name suggestions to get you started. Fellow hosts have recommended the following brands:

- Wayfair Sleep 10" Memory Foam

- Zinus 10" Green Tea Memory Foam

- Sweetnight Twilight 10" Pillowtop Memory Foam & Inner Springs Hybrid

I would caution you to not choose anything that measured less than 8-10 inches thick when purchasing mattresses. The difference in comfort is quite noticeable.

Linens and more—First off, buy a waterproof mattress protector, and have at least one spare for every other bed (in case they need washing). This can protect your mattress against most stains (urine, blood, etc.). *Never* go without a waterproof mattress protector. Buying a whole new mattress is far more costly than a $25 investment in a mattress protector! For each bed that you provide, you should have at least three complete sheet sets. I actually stock *six* sets per bed, three sets of microfiber or cotton, and three sets of flannel sheets for the winter months. There's nothing quite like the warmth of flannel sheets on a cold winter's night! I suggest having at least two blankets for each bed on the property. I use a thin waffle-weave blanket and then have an extra fluffy, warm blanket in the closet so that guests can make use of it if they wish. Allowing guests the opportunity to adjust their own bedding is the key to high marks. They want a choice. Last, for my casual/eclectic decorating style, I have found reversible quilt sets (a reversible quilt and two matching pillow shams) are perfect for my property. I have two per bed with two backups in storage for "just in case." One quilt set is in use, and the other is available in the closet should it be needed. I have seen guests use the bedding the bed comes made with, plus the extra warm blanket *and* the extra quilt. Again, choice is great, and an important thing to offer to your guests. Allow them the option to have *all* of those coverings if they so choose.

Pillows and pillow protectors—Each bed should have at least four pillows on the bed, with another two in a nearby closet. As noted above, I buy reversible quilt sets that include matching pillow shams. Two of the pillows are in pillow shams and the other two are in regular pillowcases. Most guests never need those additional pillows, but the ones that do will be incredibly grateful to you for providing them. Helpful note: Cover the spare pillows with the pillow protectors and pillowcases so they are ready to go. If you don't, some guests will use them without their pillowcases in place.

I found BioPedic pillows to be of affordable and reasonably good quality. Utopia is also a good, affordable brand. Be sure to purchase pillow protectors—enough to cover every pillow you have in stock; plus, a couple of spares should you need to wash the pillow protectors. Pillow protectors help guard against bedbugs, allergens and pet dander entering your pillows along with preventing stains. I find them well worth the investment.

Mirror (s)—Each room should have at least one mirror, preferably a full-length one, mounted on a wall or the back of the door.

Closet or wardrobe—A closet or wardrobe in which to hang clothes and possibly store extra linens is essential to every bedroom. This is also an excellent place to store a folding luggage rack, another essential for your short-term rental. Don't forget to add some hangers for guests to use.

Dresser—A dresser is recommended. Many hosts overlook this. They think it is overkill. After all, it's just a short-term stay, so why would they need it? I went to Vegas for a writer's conference in November 2021 and what was one of the first things I did? I unpacked my clothes and put them into the dresser in the hotel room. It felt nice to find my clothes easily and not have to rummage around in my suitcase. Give guests that choice. Dressers can also double as storage space for additional linens or blankets and more.

Chair—A chair is another strongly recommended piece of furniture. It's not only perfect for piling linens on when a cleaner is turning over the property, but guests appreciate having somewhere in the room to sit.

Nightstands (and more) - Another bedroom essential is a nightstand on each side of the bed. Include a digital clock (bonus points if it has built-in USB ports), a lamp on each side of the bed, at least one box of tissues, and my favorite, a pair of individually wrapped ear-plugs on each side of the bed. I include a brief note next to mine that reads *"Dear Guest—City life can be noisy, so enjoy these complimentary ear-plugs!"*

So many guests have commented on this. I also place a notepad and pen on at least one nightstand, or in a drawer. I see them used, so I know guests appreciate them!

<u>Decor and Window Treatments</u>—Keep the décor simple and muted in the bedrooms *unless* you are following a theme. Frankly, if a guest rents an STR with a *Nightmare Before Christmas* theme going on, then Jack Skellington in the bedroom probably won't give them pause. That's what they are looking for! No matter what, make sure you are using blackout curtains for any windows in rooms where guests might be sleeping. Yes, scenery is a tremendous bonus, but very few guests wish to be woken by the first rays of the sun. Fight me on this, go for it!

Utility rooms and more—A utility room, while not a central part of the STR experience, can still be incredibly useful. This is yet another reason guests choose an STR over a hotel. And again, this is your chance to shine! Most utility rooms obviously have a washer and dryer. I recommend you have the largest capacity model that you can afford. They will often do double duty in being not just for guests, but also able to handle most (if not all) the STR linens that need washing. I stock laundry soap, dryer balls (a green alternative to dryer sheets), bleach, stain treatment spray, and essential oil (for the dryer balls). The utility room is also a great place to store cleaning supplies, an ironing board, iron and clothing steamer. I also have a spare laundry basket in the utility room, as well as one centrally located in a hallway outside of the small bathroom for guest convenience. Last, include a trash can for dryer lint and more.

You may wish to set out limited quantities of laundry detergent or simply stick with inexpensive laundry detergent. Guests overuse products. If you do set out laundry pods, be sure to keep them up and out of reach of children. I added inexpensive wall décor to the utility room. Cutesy stuff that guests would like. My goal was to make my guests feel as if they were at home, or their home away from home.

Other spaces—Whether it is something as small as an enclosed back porch, a cavernous great room, or an outdoor space—think of comfort, safety, and hospitality in everything that you do while still keeping a careful eye on your bottom line. For example, I stock yoga mats, along with a book on yoga poses, on the narrow back porch. On the front porch, I have included seating, an ashtray, and a couple of tables for guests to set their phones or drinks on. Take each space in your STR, inside and out, and think of what you would want were you a guest there. Then think about what you might forget if you had been traveling with limited space in your bags.

Traveling can be tough, especially when a headache or heartburn strikes in the middle of the night. When guests know you are looking out for them, that you care enough to stock these various items, they will sing your praises and happily book with you again. Be that host!

Safety and First Aid

The safety and health of your guests is paramount. If that wasn't enough of a reason to include the basic safety and first aid items below, then your bottom line should be. Insurance companies and cities issuing STR licenses will require these items in place in order to provide insurance coverage. Without them, you risk being held liable if something were to go wrong.

Be sure each of your units has the following:

- Fire extinguisher

- Carbon monoxide and smoke detector

- Non-slip bathtub/shower stickers

- Non-slip bathmat

- Safety handle (in the shower/bathtub)

- First aid kit

- Ice/snow melt (for winter locations)

Fire extinguisher—I suggest mounting the fire extinguisher within easy reach (and in a visually obvious spot) in or around the kitchen.

Carbon monoxide and smoke detectors—Same for the carbon monoxide detectors. If you have a multi-level house, you should have at least one detector installed on every floor. Unless they are wireless and tied to the security alarm, change their batteries at least once per year.

Bathmats and More—One of the biggest dangers for any guest, is going to be slipping and falling in the bathroom. Mitigate this risk by including a non-slip mat inside of the bathtub or shower, a non-slip bathmat outside of the bathtub/shower unit, and if possible, a hospital grade safety handle inside of the shower mounted into the wall studs for extra security and safety.

First aid kit—Be sure to either mount the first aid kid kit on a wall in plain sight, or have some kind of label or sign to show where guests can find it. I typically include the following in the first aid kit:

- Adhesive tape

- Elastic wrap bandages

- Bandage strips and "butterfly" bandages in assorted sizes

- Super glue

- Gauze

- Eye shield or pad

- Tweezers

- Thermometer

- Eye wash

- Burn gel

- Calamine lotion

- Anti-diarrhea medication

- Laxative

- Antacids

- Antihistamine, such as diphenhydramine

- Hydrocortisone cream

- Cough and cold medications

- Pain relievers

<u>Ice/Snow Melt</u>—If you live in an area that becomes icy or has snow, I strongly advise you have a scraper and clearly labeled ice/snow melt where guests can clearly find them.

For your guests' health and safety, having these basics in place will not only reduce your liability but also convey the message that you care about and are concerned for their welfare and comfort while they are in your short-term rental. They are well-worth the investment!

The last thing I would suggest in this section is that your guests have all the info they need on the closest hospital, urgent care facility, and more should they have a medical need which can't be resolved through simple over-the-counter remedies. Which leads us to our next chapter, the guest handbook.

The Guest Handbook

———

E very one of your properties should have a guest handbook there in the STR. It is an essential guide to your STR property. It covers your basic rules, and it provides guests with vital information to the city or town nearest your property. Consider it a guide to all things, big and small. I provide a binder with the pages inside of plastic page protectors to help them last longer. The Guest Handbook should include:

• A welcome message - mine includes a brief message about us, along with my email address, cell phone, and our STR website.

• House rules

• House address (handy for Grubhub deliveries and more)

• Wi-Fi access

• Emergency Information—nearby hospital, including a nearby veterinary hospital, pharmacy, and even roadside assistance

• Check-in & check-out times

• Parking instructions

• Heating/cooling instructions and operation

• A basic informative review of each room. For example, I mention what we stock in the kitchen, that the stove top is gas, and that trash is picked up on Wednesdays.

• A "Before You Go" section which pretty much copies their check-out instructions

• Fun information about our city, including its founding days and fun facts.

• A list of our favorite restaurants, including dog-friendly locales (most of our guests are traveling with dogs). We list different cuisines and include breakfast, lunch, and dinner suggestions.

• Things to do, whether it is hiking, wineries, swimming, museums, or golf.

• A suggested weekend itinerary—just in case they need some ideas.

• A "thanks for staying with us," page.

Remember, you are dealing with a wide variety of guests. Some prefer reading things in print, others online, and then there are some who will just ask you directly because they don't want to plow through verbiage; they want that personal, one-on-one connection. The Guest Handbook simply helps have it all in writing, there in the entry where they are most likely to see it. Here is a link to a handy, customizable format for the STR Guest Handbook I currently use:

https://www.etsy.com/listing/1230862426. I purchased this on Etsy and then edited it using Canva. Simply download the finished product as a pdf and then print it off with a color printer. I don't have a color printer, so I use the UPS Store.

A guest handbook isn't enough, though. Next, let's talk about signs...

Signs Make the Difference

———

I t's true, many people will NOT take the time to read the Guest Handbook thoroughly, which is why you need to put up signs... everywhere.

"But wait," you might say, "you just told me how important a Guest Handbook is!"

The sad fact of the matter is, many folks will never even *touch* the Guest Handbook or even think of looking at it. That's why it's important to have signs, lots of them, for the very important information you wish to convey.

In The Cottages are signs reminding folks not to smoke, not to flush tampons and other gems down the toilet, to draw on the table in chalk, and so many more. I want to know that I've been clear, perfectly clear, about what my expectations for our guests are.

Below are some examples of signage posted throughout my property. They were usually very inexpensive to prepare—a few dollars for the frame and a sheet of printer paper in most cases, in order to convey the really important things that every guest needs to know when staying at my property. Locate the sign where it makes the most sense and try to keep them to a minimum. You don't want to overload a guest; you just want to make sure you are giving them the right information at the right time and in the right place. Here are a few examples:

Above the trash can in the kitchen—"Dear Guest—Trash days are first thing on Wednesday mornings (except following a holiday). Please take any trash out on Tuesday night and we will take care of taking it to the curb in the morning." I also have this little gem on the actual trash can. It has a bit of levity and fun, along with a gentle reminder not to break my super-cool sensor trash can. In case it isn't clear, it reads: "STOP! This trash can is magic and will open automatically if you *wave your hand over the front panel*. If you like, add a small incantation, affirmation, or just tell it to open the heck up. It's totally up to you! Please do not attempt to manually open it, as this will cause its magic motor to go *kaput*."

Next to the air plants hanging above the kitchen sink - "Dear Guest—If you are staying longer than one night, please give our friendly little air plants a spritz from the blue spray bottle below. They will appreciate it!"

On the wall above the washer and dryer in the utility room - "Dear Guest—You will probably find clean laundry in the dryer. For best efficiency, our cleaners wash the linens and then add them to the dryer before leaving. If you need to use the dryer, simply place the clean linens in the basket next to the dryer."

On the doors to the closets—"Dear Guest—You will find extra blankets and pillows inside."

Below the Nest thermostat in the living room—"Dear Guest—The Nest thermostat is set to 69 degrees year round. Any changes to it will reset back to 69 degrees at 7 a.m. Please adjust it to your preference."

Next to each bed—"Dear Guest—Upon departure, please leave any beds you have slept in un-made."

Inside of a card-holder that holds individually wrapped ear plugs—"Dear Guest—city life can be noisy at times, here are some complimentary ear plugs. Just for you!"

A free-standing 8x10 framed message on the entry table—Our About Us story (too long to post here). It describes our pesticide-free yard, complete with fruits, and veggies available for picking. It talks about how we met, our family and foster/adoptive children, our other STR offerings, and invites them to walk the yard and jump on the trampoline.

In multiple places throughout the property—Direct-booking pricing for established guests.

In the bathroom, near the shower—Instructions for using the shower on the claw-foot bathtub

I also include "No Smoking" signs in each room of the house and a green circled "Smoking Zone" outside on our front porch next to the ashtray. I absolutely detest cigarette smoke, but I understand that for many people, smoking is a way of life. No judgment, I just don't want to be under the gun to get the smell out before the next guest comes along and complains! Frankly, as a host, I think it is irrational for folks to demand that guests NOT smoke anywhere on their property. Designate a place for it, even if it is outside, as it will cause a lot less stress and tension for all parties involved.

A quick reminder of the rules, of your expectations, and of your hopes (please don't let my air plants die!) will go a long way in communicating with your guests while allowing them the personal freedom and sanctuary that they have paid good money for.

Be kind. Be upbeat. Don't do what this host has done:

Seriously? The host has the hangers counted? Or this:

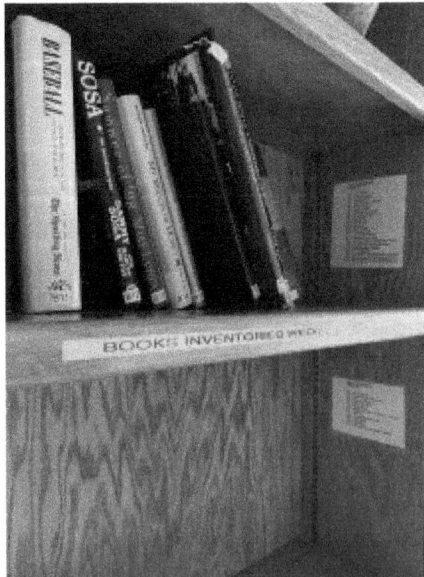

We have books scattered throughout the house. A sign near the bookshelves basically tells guests to take a book if they are in the middle of reading it, and either leave a book in its place or a "tip for the reading fairy."

Signs are wonderful ways to create a connection with your guests. Or, as with the two images above, leave a sour taste in your guest's mouth.

Now that we have covered creating the perfect space for your guests, let's talk about some of the online booking platforms, posting your first listing, and so much more. Read on!

Part IV: Bookings, Platforms, Guests

Platforms—An Overview

There are several platforms to choose from when listing your short-term rental. Keep in mind that this area is constantly changing, and with it, the companies/platforms. In an ever-changing sea of opportunity, you will see separate companies fuse, while new ones charge into the scene.

I want to discuss first why it is important to be on multiple platforms. It might seem like a hassle, but honestly, it isn't. It is simply a matter of importing and exporting a simple iCal link to your other platforms so that you don't get conflicting bookings.

While new ones are springing up all the time, I compiled the following list of short-term rental platforms in late 2022:

9flats (mainly popular in Europe)

Airbnb

Atraveo (mainly popular in Europe)

Booking.com

Casamundo

Expedia

FlipKey

Furnished Finder

HomeStay.com

HomeToGo

Hotels.com

HouseTrip

Interhome

Luxury Retreats

OneFineStay

TripAdvisor

Tripping.com

TurnKey

Vacasa

VRBO a.k.a. HomeAway

Wimdu

Of these, I have used Airbnb, Booking.com, TripAdvisor, and VRBO. The two biggest ones, at least for my area, are Airbnb and VRBO. Some companies are for luxury listings or are primarily focused on European destinations. Others require more lengthy applications to list on their platforms. With Furnished Finder, I found they are excellent if you are in the market for medical professionals (i.e., traveling nurses) and have a clear schedule for months at a time. I did not, and it was a waste of money and time to continue with them (they ask for an upfront listing fee). However, they are absolutely the way to go if you prefer a guest for longer-term stays of one to six months.

As an indie author, I promote my books through multiple bookselling platforms, including the almighty Amazon. However, having heard many horror stories of Amazon's bots suspending author's accounts for little or no reason, and their income and payouts being suspended without sufficient explanation or resources to fix it, I understand that selling wide is better. The same is true for STR owners. Occasionally, there are misunderstandings or mistruths from a disgruntled guest that could cause a listing to be suspended until an investigation is conducted. If you are listed with only a single platform, then your income is dead in the water overnight. Imagine that, for a moment. They could cancel your upcoming bookings, your payouts would be suspended, and you are completely dependent on a single booking platform as your source of revenue!

If, however, you list your property on multiple platforms; you are still in business. Don't put all of your eggs in one basket. Diversify!

Also, the big ones—Airbnb, VRBO, TripAdvisor, and Booking.com (and likely the smaller ones as well)—can provide you with the ability to share your property calendar with the other platforms in order to avoid double booking your property. This means that you can create your listings, link your calendars, and not have to worry about two different guests booking your property on two different platforms at the same time.

Each platform is different and takes a little getting used to. I would advise you get started early, though, and as you work out the kinks with listing your STR on Airbnb, immediately turn to VRBO, TripAdvisor, Booking.com (and more if you like) and begin doing the work to get listed on them and understand their unique setups.

Is Booking Direct Right for You?

First, let me clarify what I mean by booking direct, just in case it isn't clear. Booking direct means that you book off-platform, forsaking Airbnb, VRBO, and others. You may use Venmo, Paypal, Zelle, other peer-to-peer payment platforms, or cash. With it, as with most things, comes pros and cons.

Pros	Cons
You keep all of the fees* (unless you accept credit cards, which usually carry a small transaction fee)	If there is a dispute on a credit card, you may be out the entire reservation fee
Attract your ideal guest	More responsibility and no customer service team to handle it or act as an intermediary
Managing your calendar may be easier	No host guarantee for damages
You can get more info about your guests that you would normally not get through an online booking site	Can cost to run the hosting software on your own website
Can demand a security deposit	Less traffic visibility (no platform advertising for you if you go 100% direct booking)

There are some significant concerns I have with the potential drawbacks of direct booking. As a result, I have chosen a hybrid approach. I advertise in the units that I allow for direct bookings from established guests only and offer them a rate that is usually less than what they paid through Airbnb or VRBO. Airbnb especially, since they add on a 15% service fee for guests, whereas they charge hosts 3%. I will typically offer an average of 10% off of what they paid through Airbnb, which means my potential income is 5-8% higher with a direct booking, depending on whether they pay via credit card. The first year I did this was 2021 and 1.41% of my income came from direct bookings. By the 4th quarter of 2022, I saw that number rise to 4.35%. It isn't a lot, and that is fine. New guests must go through Airbnb or one of the other major online booking platforms and this helps me winnow out any I would NOT want to come back.

I personally would suggest waiting at least six months to a year before rolling out the option for direct bookings. Get a solid feel for your market and your guests and then decide on whether you wish to accept bookings directly.

One other point, before we move on. Under no circumstances should you ever solicit a guest on one of the major platforms to make a direct booking with you. That will get you banned from the platform, as it is not only a conflict of interest, but a violation of their terms of service. So don't do it!

Next up, posting your first STR listing...

Posting Your Listing on Airbnb

———

I'm going to cover how to post your listing on Airbnb using their current quick list model and then dig into the weeds in the following chapter. It can be relatively easy to do the initial posting, but here are a lot of details that Airbnb leaves out, details you can only access *after* you have posted your listing.

Before we dive in, however, I'm going to give you a quick and easy link: http://www.airbnb.com/r/strsuccess

This takes you through my affiliate referral link. There are no fees for you, nor is any of your income funneled to me, only a $40 bonus for you from Airbnb, and a referral bonus to me for referring you as a new host. It is a win-win for both of us!

By the end of this chapter, you should have your basic listing live on Airbnb. The following chapter will dig into the details and get it just the way you want it. But for now, let's just get the basic listing up and operational.

If you haven't researched your immediate area, now is the time to do it. You can fill out the Predicting Income worksheet in the Complete STR Financial Tracking spreadsheet. This file is available for free download at my author website:

https://www.christineshuck.com/str-success-resources

Before posting your first listing, you need to know what you want to accept in terms of:

- Nightly fees

- Cleaning fees

- Minimum and maximum lengths of stay

There is an extremely informative video on pricing cleaning fees by Sean Rakidzich, the driving force (and brilliant mind) behind Airbnb Automated. He gives a very comprehensive explanation of it here:

https://www.youtube.com/watch?v=CDrrogSVz-U

As for the minimum and maximum lengths of stay, I recommend reviewing *Part I: Short-Term? Mid-Term? Long-Term?* if you still have questions on that.

At the onset of your short-term rental experience, you will probably receive a majority of your business from Airbnb since it is the largest (at least here in the United States) with VRBO following shortly behind. However, as I mentioned earlier, it is important to not put all your eggs in one basket. Set up your listing on Airbnb, familiarize yourself with the platform, and then branch out to others. This is perfectly acceptable to do; in fact, it is expected. All the major booking platforms allow you to import and export your STR calendar to all the other platforms in order to not have a double booking occur.

So here is the quick and dirty on posting your first listing with Airbnb:

Again, if you do not already have an account, create one by following my referral link here: www.airbnb.com/r/strsuccess[1]. This also has the bonus of adding $40 to your pocket. It's a win-win for you and me!

Click on the link above and you should see a page similar to this...

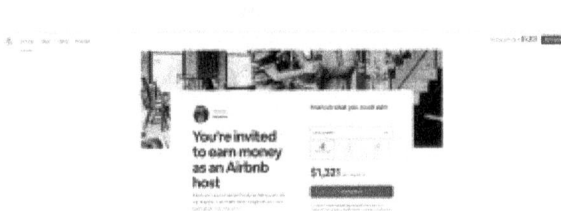

---

1. http://www.airbnb.com/r/strsuccess

Click on the Get Started button and it will take you to a quick and easy page that reads "Become a Host in 10 easy steps." It actually has eleven sections, but hey, who's counting?!

And here are the ~~ten~~ *eleven* easy steps...

1. *What kind of place will you host?* (apartment, house, secondary unit, unique space, bed-and-breakfast, boutique hotel)—In most cases, you will list either an apartment or house. If you have something unique, like we do in the Hedy Lamarr Vintage Airstream, then choose Unique Space.

2. *Which of these best describes your space?*—Depending on how you answered the first question, you should now have a list of choices that will narrow down exactly what your STR offering matches best. Try to be as accurate as possible.

3. *What kind of space will guests have?*—An entire place, a private room, or a shared room are the typical choices.

4. *The street address*—Don't worry, guests won't see this until they have made payment, the booking is confirmed, and it is the day of the reservation.

5. *How many guests would you like to welcome?*—Be prepared to specify the total number of guests, how many beds you are providing, the number of bedrooms (since there can be more than one bed in a bedroom), and the number of bathrooms. I list a max of six guests and state clearly that there are two beds and two couches. Note: they consider bathrooms that only contain a sink and toilet half baths.

6. *Let guests know what your place offers*—Airbnb provides a plethora of boxes to check. From amenities such as a pool, hot tub, BBQ grill, fire pit, pool table, and more. As well as guest favorites, like a dedicated workspace and safety equipment (first aid kit, smoke alarm, fire extinguisher, etc.)

7. *Add some photos of your place*—I go into detail on this in the next chapter. For now, post one picture as your placeholder, but plan on adding more photos as you progress through the next chapter's

115

detailed instructions.

8. *Let's give your place a name*—Cottage West (which is on the west end of our properties) and Hedy Lamarr Airstream (named after a truly brilliant actress), were the initial names of our two STRs. However, as you progress through the next chapter, the *Listing Title* section may change that to something else. Don't worry, you are not stuck with the name, and can change it later on. There is a helpful article with tips on writing a great Listing Title here: http://bit.ly/3Vu1UsV.

9. *Describe your place*—Airbnb limits you to 500 characters for this. Look at my suggestions below in *Listing description*. You can also see what I have written for one of my properties there. Later, after you have submitted your listing, you can go back and add to this section under the Listing section in Airbnb. Click Edit and you will find *The Space* that allows for over 500 characters. Fill this out with all the details your little heart desires. Airbnb understands that most people want information in small accessible little bites. That's why they limit the listing title to 50 characters, or the basic property description to 500 characters. There are others, though, who want to know more about a property before booking, so give them as much detail as possible.

10. *Pricing*—You've done your research, so this should be a straightforward decision. If, however, you skipped that part back in Part 1, now is the time to do it. You can find the spreadsheet in Complete STR Financial Tracking spreadsheet. This file is available for free download at my website: https://www.christineshuck.com/str-success-resources. You may notice that Airbnb doesn't give you the option to list a cleaning fee. I suspect they are hoping you won't. Don't worry, you can edit this in later. For now, simply put in the nightly price your data shows you can get. Also, you have a choice to make. Will you offer a 20% discount to your first three guests? This can help you get booked faster. You are also likely going to host folks who are looking for a deal. It's up to you. I did it for my first STR and not for my second. My second STR is unique, however, and I adjust my pricing significantly during the off-season already.

When I rolled it out, it was the beginning of the busy season and I wanted to earn as much as possible with it while the getting was good. I didn't see any significant difference in bookings to warrant extending a 20% off price.

11. *Disclosures*—The last step in this quick and easy listing is to disclose whether you have any of the following: security cameras, weapons, or dangerous animals. Just click the boxes as they apply.

Once you have done this, and clicked *Review Your Listing*, you can now see how your STR will look to the average guest scrolling on their phone. You can publish your listing, then go into your account and edit for the rest of the details. I recommend you do this right away.

In the next chapter, I go into exhaustive detail through every part of your listing that you will want to consider now that you are up and live. It truly was exhausting to write, and is my longest chapter. That said, I highly recommend you go through it, anyway!

Editing and Refining Your Listing on Airbnb

N ow that you have gone through the basic steps, let's refine and add details to the listing so that everything is as complete as possible. Airbnb makes it easy to get started, but they also don't want to get into the nitty-gritty details—especially those pesky little details like cleaning fees, cancellation policies, and Instant Book settings. But those areas are important to hosts, *very* important. If you want to control who is booking your property, when they can cancel (hopefully not at the last minute for a full refund), or whether you get paid cleaning fees, then you will want to go into your hosting account on Airbnb, click on Menu, and then Listings, and go through each of the areas step-by-step.

You should see your listing organized as follows:

- Listing details

- Pricing and availability

- Policies and rules

- Info for guests

- Co-hosts

Under these main headings, there are more sub-menus and we are going to take them in turn. Let's start with Photos...

Photos

Your best foot in the metaphorical door will be your photos, so let's make sure they are good ones! Keep the following in mind as you accumulate them:

- Look at other comparable listings' photos and compare

- Use as high-quality of a camera as possible

- Consider hiring a professional photographer

- Use *landscape*, not portrait setting for your photos whenever possible

- Use the biggest draw to your property as the first photo (with Cottage West I used the vintage claw-foot bathtub, filled with bubbles)

- Your first five photos are the most important—choose them wisely

- Keep your target market in mind

- Don't include images of items NOT in your listing (for instance, a host who showed a video arcade game that wasn't actually IN the property) or if you do, label the photo clearly (i.e., "Arcade games available in nearby clubhouse of complex").

- Take photos where everything is staged, clean, and ready (no mess!)

- Try taking photos with curtains open and closed, to see which looks better

- Showcase your property's unique attributes

- Include interior and exterior photos and even close-ups of attractive décor details (Tree of Life table)

- Caption the photos (Bedroom 1, Bedroom 2, etc.)

Here is an example of my Cottage West listing:

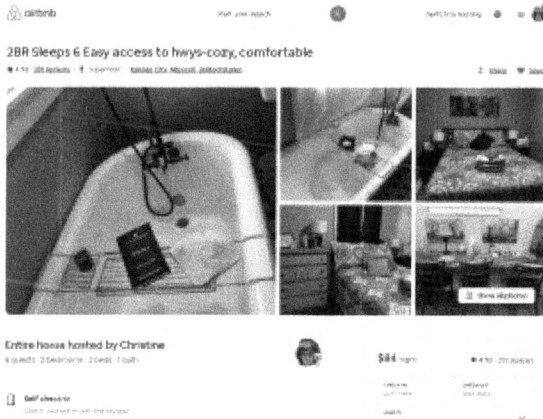

After that, in later photos, I do a full walk-through in photos of the house starting with the front porch, moving into the front entry/living room, adding in clips of hand-written as well as official reviews from happy guests as I go, showing off the artistic touches, amenities (a desk, washer and dryer, charging station, and more), and the small and big details as a guest would see them as they move through the house.

A final note on photos: Update, Update, Update!—Whenever you make changes, update the photos on the listing. If a chair gets swapped out, or a slipcover added, take new photos and update them on the site. Even if they are improvements, guests hate surprises. They want what they saw in the photos, no more, and certainly no less. I received a couple of less-than-stellar reviews complaining that I had changed the furniture after I swapped out a chair and added a slipcover to a couch damaged by a guest's dog. The couch was a marked change in appearance (brown chenille to red and cream floral) that, despite it being only the slipcover that changed, the guest thought it was different furniture entirely. Differences from the photos and reviews noting such things lead future guests to be suspicious and move on, fearing they are being misled.

In a world where photos are airbrushed, cropped, and altered—it is easy to give the appearance of something being better when it is not. And I get that,

I really do. In March 2020, I booked an Airbnb in Bath, England. The photo of the front of the property was of a completely different building, and that wasn't the only misleading part of the listing! People want what they have seen in the photos and nothing else will do. Save yourself a poor review and make sure the photos are up to date at all times.

Listing Basics

Listing title—Your listing title (along with that ever-important primary picture) is the first glance potential guests will have at your property, so it had better be good. Consider:

- Audience appeal—Why does a guess want to book *your* STR? Who is your target audience? Consider a title that will appeal to the needs and expectations of your typical guests. Use words that appeal to your ideal guest, 'secluded' or 'romantic' if you are hoping for honeymooners. 'Convenient' or 'modern' or 'bright' if targeting business travelers.

- Make the most of the character limit—Most platforms allow up to 50 characters for a title, so use all 50!

- Use abbreviations and symbols to save characters—With becomes w/, bedroom becomes BR, air conditioning becomes A/C, and so on. There are many who are using emojis as well. I think this works especially well with the under 40 age brackets. I, old fuddy duddy that I am, cannot stand the things, but I recognize that there is an enormous set of potential clients I may miss out on by not using them in my listing title.

- Avoid using generic words in your title—Toss out great, nice and good and embrace eclectic, insta-worthy, renovated, green, enviro-friendly, and more.

- Don't use all caps—Using all capital letters is the same as shouting. No one wants to hear about your SUPER

SCHMANCY FIVE BEDROOM VILLA. They just don't. No screaming; you aren't a barker.

• Highlight the best features—If you aren't sure, take your friends or neighbors through the property and ask them for a list of words. If you have been in business for a while, look at the reviews folks have left—what do they say? Thinking about this made me edit my title to read: *Cottage West-Close to everything, cozy, and clean.* Later on, I briefly tried out *2BR Sleeps 6 Easy access to hwys-cozy, comfortable,* but it didn't strike the right chord.

• Mention nearby landmarks or appealing destinations—We are just a 15-minute drive from the stadiums (football and baseball), as well as less than a five-minute drive from the jazz district, and Kansas City's Power and Light district.

Listing description—You have already done this. Click Edit anyway, as there is a sub-menu of choices. You can leave this as is or tweak your wording while you are here. Here is an example of what I have written for Cottage West:

We have thought of every detail. You are HOME!

Cottage West has...
Lounge in a gorgeous claw foot bathtub!
Bedroom 1 - queen bed.
Bedroom 2 - full bed that guests have described as "the best night's sleep [they] have ever had."
2 Couches in living room
Kid friendly
Pet friendly
54" Roku TV w/Netflix, Hulu & more.
A back porch for sipping coffee or practicing yoga and front porch for smokers. Fully stocked. From kitchen spices & pantry essentials, a coffee/tea station, even a washer & dryer.

I had listed in the listing title that we could sleep six, but I really wanted to make sure I clarified that. There are two beds, a full and a queen, and in a pinch, the couches can serve as beds as well, allowing for up to 6 guests. I also wanted to clarify, since searches on Airbnb are limited and don't seem to include finding a pet-friendly house, that we are indeed pet-friendly. Speaking of pets, we are also kid-friendly. That's a joke, folks. I have kids of my own! I'm trying to pack in the amenities as much as possible since I'm limited to the 500 characters.

The space—Finally! Over 500 characters are allowed! Time to roll out the charm, folks! You didn't have this option in the setup, so now you can add it. Here is what I have written for Cottage West:

This fully renovated 1910 bungalow with warm, inviting colors throughout comes fully stocked with everything you need during your stay.

The two bedrooms are cozy and comfortable. All linens are included (cool microfiber sheets in the summer, scrumptious flannel in the winter), digital clocks with USB ports, ample storage space, and luggage racks. The two couches (one squishy, one firm) in the living room provide additional sleep possibilities beyond the two bedrooms for a total of six guests.

The bathroom includes an antique claw-foot bathtub with a classy shower conversion (seriously though, take a soak, you'll love it!).

There is a utility room with a washer and dryer and laundry soap, as well as an ironing board, a portable fan, a pack 'n' play and a high chair that attaches to the table for folks with little ones. Kids' dish sets are also available.

The kitchen is complete with a 1930s era Roper gas stove (stove top only—the oven is NOT functional), toaster oven, microwave, spices, cookware, and all kinds of fun freebies in the pantry. Eat at the blackboard-finish table, which has room for four chairs, and draw a picture!

In the living room you will find ample desk space at the large Tree of Life table (hand drawn and stained by the owner) as well as a charger, couch, and chairs where you can watch TV (Netflix, Hulu, Amazon Prime, and Curiosity Stream included).

In nicer weather, you may wish to sit on the front porch in the vintage glider or enjoy the enclosed back porch and sip coffee or practice yoga/meditation.

Guests are free to enjoy the very large, shared fenced yard (yes, you are welcome to jump on the trampoline) and we are pet-friendly (no additional fees for pets).

We ask that you keep your pets leashed, as this is a shared yard. Want to know more? Ask away!

<u>Guest access</u>—Here you can let the guests know which parts of the space they can access. Here is what I've written for Cottage West:

All of the main floor of the house is available. The attic and basement are off-limits. In addition, feel free to roam through the yard to the east of the Cottage West. We have fruit trees, a fire pit, a large pond, a trampoline, and plenty of flowers to enjoy!

<u>Other details to note</u>—Any special info you want your guests to know? Write it here. Again, I've provided an example from Cottage West...

1. *Pets—pets are welcome, no extra fees for their stay. We expect they be crated in a kennel when left alone or if they are not house trained. Please be a responsible pet owner. All pets must be leashed when outside.*
2. *Smoking—Cottage West is a smoke-free home. Take it outside to the front porch or out in the yard. Violators will receive a one-star review and a $100 fine.*
3. *Parties—Absolutely NO PARTIES at Cottage West. We have young children, and there are hard-working families who live in this neighborhood. We will remove violators from the premises and not receive a refund for their stay.*

<u>Number of guests</u>—Here's your chance to change the total number of guests allowed.

<u>Custom link</u>—This is a super-cool option that Airbnb rolled out. Would you like to give folks an easy link to your STR? You can create it here! For Cottage West, the link is: **https://airbnb.com/h/cottagewest**. It's a little more personal than your space URL.

<u>Languages</u>—You can list what languages you speak here, or it will default to the standard for the country you are located in. In my case, English.

CHRISTINE D. SHUCK

Listing status—If you ever want to suspend or snooze your listing, here is where you will do it. Airbnb also offers simple explanations of your different options.

● Listed
Guests can find your listing in search results and request or book available dates.

☾ Snoozed
Remove your listing from search results for a set period of time.

● Unlisted
Guests can't book your listing or find it in search results.

⊘ Deactivate
Permanently remove your listing from Airbnb.

Amenities

What amenities do you offer? Here, you can really dig down into the weeds and go beyond the few listed in the original ten steps. Make sure this section is filled out completely and accurately. Be very specific. Do you have window units for your air conditioning or central air? Guaranteed, you will get a complaint if you don't mention that loud window unit! The same goes for the heating; don't hide the fact you have a portable space heater (say it in the description), otherwise, you risk a horrible review from someone who didn't want to wait an hour or more for the space to heat. In the same vein, a hot plate and mini-fridge is NOT a kitchen, just as a dedicated workspace must have an available electrical outlet and not be on an already overloaded circuit (I live in an old house, so I know how these things can go!).

For home safety, do not forget to add a first aid kit, fire extinguisher, carbon monoxide alarm and smoke alarm to your property. These are musts, unless you want something awful to happen and to be sued for every penny you are worth. When lives are at stake, do the right thing!

As you move into the different areas, consider putting a reminder in your calendar to go through your listing every couple of months. Things change and you want to stay current. As I went through the amenities section, I found plenty of amenities that I offer that weren't listed as options before. I checked quite a few!

Under Parking and Transportation, please note that "free parking on premises" is NOT the same as "free street parking" Early on, I made the mistake of checking both of them yes, when actually to park off of the street (i.e. behind our locked gate) was technically *possible*, at the time we had not put in the gravel driveway or installed the curb cut. It meant parking on grass after having to drive over a curb. A guest read "free parking on premises" and then was unhappy with the street parking option. He said nothing until after, so his review was slightly less than all five stars. We have fixed this and guests love having the driveway and double gates that close. It gives them a feeling of security that street parking does not.

Location

<u>Address</u>—This should already show the correct address

<u>Neighborhood description</u>—This is a great opportunity to tell guests about your neighborhood and its benefits

<u>Getting around</u>—Since we are in a city, I give potential guests options such as Uber, Lyft, and that they know about our free light rail service in the downtown area.

<u>Location sharing</u>—Here you can opt in or out of sharing your exact address. I recommend using the General Location option for security. You don't need a guest showing up before a scheduled reservation or releasing your specific address to people who have no intention of renting from you and instead want to burglarize or even squat in your home. You can send your specific address to your guests on the day of reservation instead.

<u>Scenic views</u>—Click Edit and you will see an extensive list. You can mark multiple choices here.

Property and rooms

Property type—You have already filled this one out.

Rooms and spaces—Here you can identify the different rooms, and include pictures, so that a potential guest has a better idea of which rooms are which.

Accessibility

If your space is accessible for those with mobility issues, here is the perfect place to let folks know! Our properties are older, and therefore inaccessible for those with significant mobility issues. However, if you own a more modern property, this is your chance to stand out from the crowd! There is a market, to be sure, so go for it, and drop me an email and let me know how your business grows as a result!

Guest Safety

Click Edit and look at this section. You have already filled some of it out in the quick start, but now you can fill in some details. For example, as I was running through it and writing this section, I realized I didn't have the trampoline listed under Climbing or Play Structure, so I added:

"There is a trampoline with safety netting in the shared yard that guests are welcome to use at their own risk."

I also noticed that the pond we installed last year was also not listed, so I added:

"There is a pond on the property that is approximately 3-5 feet in depth."

Under Safety Devices, I added the following explanation to the Security Cameras section:

"Ring doorbell camera and two Ring motion sensor w/floodlight cameras—one that monitors the front porch and the other that monitors the back of Cottage West. These devices are motion-activated and record any movement outside for crime and safety purposes only."

The clarification under the Ring devices is very important. If you are going to have any kind of security devices, and honestly, I think you should, then I recommend: 1) you only have them outside of your property, never inside, 2) that you disclose where they are and, 3) why you have them there. Not disclosing the cameras can get your account suspended. And not explaining the reason for their existence can cause guests to be wary and even paranoid about your motivations.

Pricing

Nightly price—Here you can set a base price. You likely already did it in the initial setup, but you could change it here if you wished to. You can also turn on Smart Pricing and have Airbnb determine the best nightly price possible for your region. I will warn you, however, that their prices are rather low. I suggest you set your own price once you have completed your research on the surrounding area, your competition, etc.

Listing currency—no need to change this, guests will see prices in their own currency.

Discounts—I've mentioned it before, but I actually prefer shorter stays. I make more money at it since I'm the one doing the cleanings. That said, I have a 5% weekly discount and a 15% monthly discount set in place. You can also set Custom Length of Stay discounts, Early Bird discounts, and last-minute discounts.

Cleaning fee—Here you can delineate between a regular cleaning fee and a short-stay cleaning fee. My cleaning fees are pretty low right now. After all, I can clean my little two-bedroom, one-bath in approximately 45 minutes (this includes washing the linens and putting them in the dryer), so a $50 short-stay cleaning fee more than adequately pays for my time, and the $65 regular cleaning fee (for anything longer than two nights) is usually enough to cover any extra time I take to get the STR up to snuff. Before you fill this section out, and if you are hiring cleaning staff, get a quote first, so you aren't hit with sticker shock. A cleaning crew can be pricey, and you want excellent service out of them every single time they clean. Do not assume that just because someone cleans houses, they will work for a measly $10-$15 an hour, because you definitely will get what you pay for and your guests will be merciless in their reviews!

Pet fee—You can list a pet fee here. This is not a per-pet fee, simply an inclusive pet fee. If you charge $20 for a pet fee, the guest will pay $20, whether they have one dog or five. And, as noted by Airbnb, and as legislated by the Americans with Disabilities Act, a guest does not have to pay a pet fee for a *service animal* (note I didn't say *emotional support animal*). I charge a token amount of $10. It isn't a large amount, but most pet owners expect some kind of fee. For those who don't tell me they are bringing a pet, I don't pursue it. It isn't worth it, honestly.

Linens fee—Perhaps your area differs from mine, but in my case, I do not make use of this fee. Linens are usually considered part of the rental. However, in other countries, or in some isolated regions, this might not be the case. Unless you have heard specifically about other local hosts charging a linens fee, I would not recommend placing any fee here. Yes, linens require washing and that costs money in water and detergent, and yes, you might have a service do them for you if you have a larger place. This is a personal decision you need to make. It is also a line item that would be listed out in the charges detail and that a potential guest would see and possibly question.

Resort fee—Only charge a resort fee if your property is in a resort and they charge a per-reservation fee

Management fee—This is not a fee I would charge to a guest. You must make your own judgment on it. Compare the charges of those around you for a better understanding of what is expected and what is not.

Community fee—This is not a fee I would charge to a guest. You must make your own judgment on it. Compare the charges of those around you for a better understanding of what is expected and what is not.

Extra guest fee—I don't charge an extra guest fee and I will explain why...

1. My time spent cleaning is essentially the same, whether one person

uses the property or five. It might vary by as much as 15-20 minutes extra for extra guests, but often it doesn't. So why charge more for more guests? This might be very different for you, however.

2. An additional per-guest fee encourages guests to lie about how many are in their party. It is a human condition to get away with less, if possible. And do you really want to argue with a guest or watch their comings and goings on a camera and try to count heads? It's a disaster in the making.

3. Potentially fewer bookings if you have a pricey additional guest fee in place.

4. A guest is pissed they got caught and angry you would ask them to pay more. They are also embarrassed at being caught. Imagine how teenagers act when they are caught doing something they shouldn't. Adults aren't much different, just more hostile and capable of leaving nit-picky, negative reviews.

It's up to you. If you really want to deal with policing your guests, following up and arguing, cajoling or guilting them into being honest, then by all means go ahead and charge a per-guest fee. Yes, you might make a decent sum, but at what cost?

Weekend nightly price—If you prefer to "fix it and forget it" you may wish to have a standard weekend nightly price which will override your weeknight pricing, set up when you first posted your listing. Weekend rates are typically higher and better earners for most STR hosts, myself included. Again, my rates are on the low end of things, so I keep my rates at $99 per night base rate across the board, and then adjust them down the week of, or sometimes one to two weeks ahead of time to ensure I'm getting maximum capacity in my properties.

Taxes

Airbnb collects and remits any applicable occupancy taxes on your behalf. This is worth double-checking on the other platforms as well to make sure they are doing the same thing. However, any state or federal personal income taxes you may incur are your responsibility to report and pay on your own. I recommend setting aside a minimum of 15% of your gross income towards this eventuality. More on this in *Part VII: Money Matters*.

Trip Length

Minimum stay—I have a one-night stay minimum, but I recommend you click on *Edit*, and then on *Customize minimum stay requirements* for additional options. For instance, you may wish to not have to pay cleaners extra, or clean on most weekends, so you ask for a two-night minimum on Fridays, for example. Or perhaps you are always busy on Tuesdays and cannot handle cleaning the STR that day, so you could instead mark a 2-night minimum for anyone staying on Monday nights. It's a handy feature.

Maximum stay—If, for example, your city or state confers renter's rights upon any guest who stays longer than 30 days, and you don't want to deal with trying to evict someone, you may wish to set a maximum stay to 28 or 29 days. I have mine set at 28 nights, just in case.

Custom trip lengths—Here you can set trip length and check-in day requirements for specific dates.

Calendar Availability

Advance notice—Do you need advance notice of a guest's arrival? Here is the place to request it. I have set it for Same Day, and I allow guests to book until 8 P.M. I always have the properties ready, and I am often asleep by 9 p.m., sometimes earlier, so I don't miss a reservation request. You can change this, however, to give you one, two, three and even seven days' notice.

Preparation time—How much preparation time will you need to get the STR ready for more guests? Your choices are 1) None, 2) Block one night before and after each reservation, or 3) Block two nights before and after each reservation. I chose None, because of my proximity to our STRs and my ability to clean the properties in the three-hour window between when a guest leaves and when the next one arrives.

Availability window—How many months in advance are you willing to book guests? I have *All future dates* selected, but I also have a team in place for when I go on vacation that handles my cleanings, while I handle the customer service side of things.

If you aren't sure that will work for you, choose something that will.

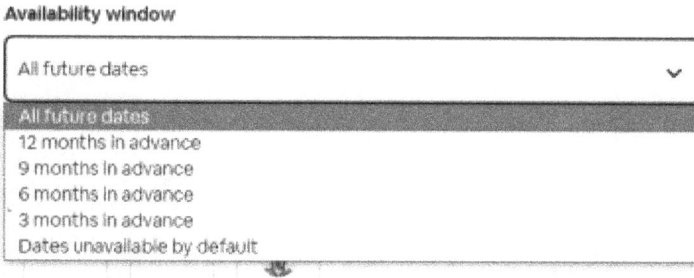

Availability window

All future dates ⌄

All future dates
12 months in advance
9 months in advance
6 months in advance
3 months in advance
Dates unavailable by default

Restricted check-in days—Here is another way to restrict guests from staying on certain days of the week. You can restrict a guest from checking in on a Wednesday if, for example, you prefer one-on-one check-in and are gone out of town every Wednesday.

The other thing to keep in mind regarding availability, and that is what I can only describe as "party days."

Here in our area, those would be:

• 4th of July

• Halloween

• New Year's Eve

Yes, there are plenty of other holidays, but those three are bad news. We block them off on our calendars. It simply isn't worth hosting on those days. I'll talk later about screening guests, but let's just say that, despite our best efforts, locals have booked our properties in the past and created problems. It was enough of a lesson for me. I now block off the days far in advance.

If you live in a tourist hub, this might not work for you. You might think, "Those could be my busiest days!" So take my advice with a grain of salt. For us, in a city, those three days of the year are nothing but problems and I'm unwilling to put myself through a sleepless night (2020's New Year's Eve included some fool emptying a clip into the air right next to our daughter's room) just for one night's income.

What are you comfortable with in terms of availability? This goes hand in hand with your own availability to oversee your STR, or have another person or service handling it. If you are outsourcing it, are they available seven days a week, 365 days a year? Are there any limitations a property manager or co-host will have when making sure your STR is cared for properly?

Calendar Sync

Here is where you can link the calendars from Airbnb, VRBO, TripAdvisor, and Booking.com. To do so, you will need to first create your accounts on these sites, one at a time. Import and export the .ical calendars for each booking site you are now listed on, and this will prevent guests on one platform from booking when you the property is already occupied through another booking platform. Very handy! I tend to just use my Airbnb calendar, since that will show me the other platform bookings. If I have a direct booking, I block the day on my Airbnb calendar and add a note of the guest's name for my reference. It automatically blocks that day on all the other calendars.

Sharing Settings

Find out more about the listings your potential guests are checking out. If you share some details about your listing and bookings with other hosts, you can see the listings that guests end up booking after checking out your place.

Policies and Rules

We are done with pricing and availability and now we finally get to move on to policies and rules. This is an especially important section regarding your cancellation policies and the Instant Book feature.

Policies

<u>Standard cancellation policy</u>—What kind of cancellation policy you choose is a very important one. Let's look at your choices:

○ Flexible
Full refund 1 day prior to arrival

○ Flexible or Non-refundable
In addition to Flexible, offer a non-refundable option—guests pay 10% less, but you keep your payout no matter when they cancel. **Learn more**

● Moderate
Full refund 5 days prior to arrival

○ Moderate or Non-refundable
In addition to Moderate, offer a non-refundable option—guests pay 10% less, but you keep your payout no matter when they cancel. **Learn more**

○ Firm NEW
Full refund for cancellations up to 30 days before check-in. If booked fewer than 30 days before check-in, full refund for cancellations made within 48 hours of booking and at least 14 days before check-in. After that, 50% refund up to 7 days before check-in. No refund after that.

○ Firm or Non-refundable NEW
In addition to Firm, offer a non-refundable option—guests pay 10% less, but you keep your payout no matter when they cancel. **Learn more**

○ Strict
Full refund for cancellations made within 48 hours of booking, if the check-in date is at least 14 days away. 50% refund for cancellations made at least 7 days before check-in. No refunds for cancellations made within 7 days of check-in.

○ Strict or Non-refundable
In addition to Strict, offer a non-refundable option—guests pay 10% less, but you keep your payout no matter when they cancel. **Learn more**

As you can see, I prefer the moderate cancellation policy. I dislike any choices that include non-refundable. Guests abuse this. They go for the cheaper price and then try to squirm out of the non-refundable side of things. I found it far easier to give them no 10% discount and allow cancellations up to seven days prior to the start of the reservation. Having the non-refundable discount was more interaction-intensive and more work, with less income. Know that you can change this should it become necessary. When you do, however, it affects only new reservations, *not* reservations that guests have already made.

Long-term cancellation policy—This is a newer feature for Airbnb and a good one. You might be more flexible on the cancellation of a stay that is a few days or a week, but when a guest schedules your property for 28 nights or longer, and then wants to cancel, that can have long-lasting effects, especially if your calendar has been showing as booked and unavailable for any length of time.

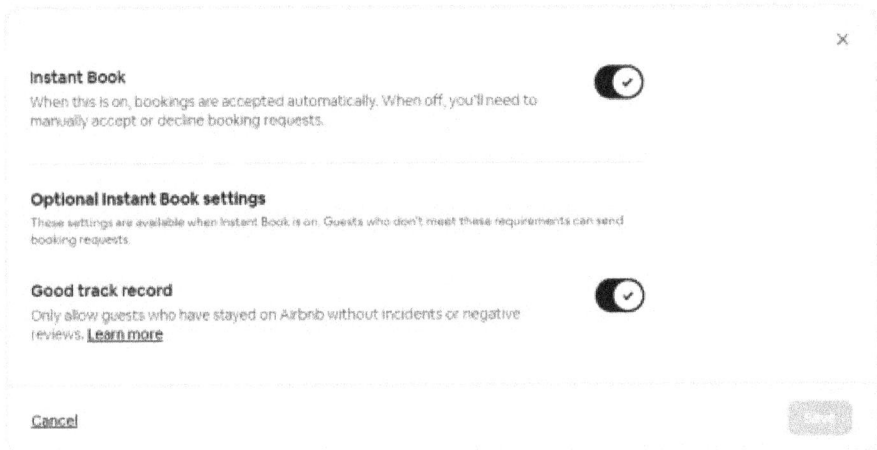

Instant Book
When this is on, bookings are accepted automatically. When off, you'll need to manually accept or decline booking requests.

Optional Instant Book settings
These settings are available when Instant Book is on. Guests who don't meet these requirements can send booking requests.

Good track record
Only allow guests who have stayed on Airbnb without incidents or negative reviews. **Learn more**

Cancel

Instant Book—One choice Airbnb would prefer you choose is Instant Book. I recommend using Instant Book. It pushes your property higher in the Airbnb algorithm. Definitely double check one *thing, though. Click Edit and check yes for "Good track record". If other hosts have had difficulties* with the guest, they won't be able to instant book with you.

Check-in window—What time do you want to allow your guests to arrive? I actually try to match what most hotels offer, which is a 2 p.m. (or later) arrival time. I leave my guest's end time for check-in as flexible. Most of my guests are driving through and their arrival time can vary tremendously based on weather and traffic conditions.

Checkout time—What time do you need your guests to leave by? I set an 11 a.m. checkout time. Again, I'm attempting to mimic hotel rules here. Eventually, when I have all four properties up and running, I may need to alter both the checkout and check-in times to provide a larger window for all the cleanings to be done. For now, having a window of 11 a.m. to 2 p.m. for cleaning allows me to get it done easily and not feel under the gun.

House Rules

Suitable for children (2-12 years)—Is your house suitable for children?

Suitable for infants (under 2 years)—Is your house suitable for infants?

Pets allowed—Will you be allowing pets? Note: You cannot disallow service animals. More on this in *Part II: Pets? Yes or No?*

Smoking allowed—Most STR hosts do not allow smoking inside of the units. However, you have the option of allowing it, and that is totally up to you. I imagine that could be quite the bonus for smokers to be allowed to smoke inside of a property.

Events allowed—Unless you have a home that is remote and capable of hosting family gatherings or weddings, I would advise that you not allow events. Airbnb, as well as other platforms, strictly prohibit parties. Not that they prevent all event gatherings, just those deemed as parties.

Additional rules—Here is space for you to list any rules you might have that have not been covered in other areas. I chose to re-state several rules, and here is an example from my Cottage West listing:

Pets must be crated if left alone on the property. Guests will be held financially responsible for any damage by their pets. Pets must stay leashed in the yard as it is a shared space. Absolutely NO smoking inside of home, a $100 extra cleaning fee will apply to any violators of this rule.

Guest Requirements

<u>Profile photo required</u>—You can request that the guest have a profile photo already on file. You cannot see it until after the booking is confirmed, however.

Laws and Regulations

<u>Local laws</u>—This serves as a reminder to hosts that different municipalities have different laws regarding short-term rentals and you should know what your particular local laws are.

<u>Primary use of listing</u>—Choose between "the space is primarily set up for guests," and "I keep personal belongings in the space."

Info for Guests

This section mostly re-iterates information already filled out. It is information the guest sees on their end.

<u>Pre-booking details</u>—The check-in window you already filled out above, and the check-out time should be the same. Here you can add your guidebook if you wish. You can include places (restaurants, points of interest), describe the neighborhood, add fun information about your city or town, or traveler advice inside of it. Last, *Interaction with guests* gives you a couple of options to choose from. Here is what I chose, and what I wrote, for guests to read:

Interaction with guests

Tell guests if you'll be available to offer help throughout their stay and how you'll keep in touch with them.

○ I plan to socialize with my guests

● I give my guests space but am available when needed

○ I won't be available in person

I live next door in the brick house. You can reach me by calling, texting, email, or by knocking on our door if you need anything. If it is after 9pm and you have any difficulty accessing the space, please press the Ring doorbell and it will sound inside of our house and we will wake up and help. We would love to meet you, but we also respect your privacy!

Post-booking details—Once booked, a guest will receive your address, directions, and house manual on the day of, or the day before, a reservation. Just double-check the address listed to make sure it matches correctly. Under *Directions*, I suggest choosing the nearest highway or major intersection and giving basic directions from there. These days, with GPS, it is rarely needed, but also important to have all the information you can make available to your guests.

For the house manual, I once again reiterate a few points, just to make sure guests have seen them. Here is an example from Cottage West:

House manual

We want your stay to be comfortable and refreshing. Cottage West was designed with the traveler, and your every possible need in mind. You will find analgesics and over-the-counter remedies in the medicine cabinet in the bathroom, cookware and utensils in the kitchen, and extra linens in the bedrooms should you need them. We want you to enjoy your stay!

We do have a few rules, however:

-No smoking (we utilize FreshAir sensor technology) or vaping inside of the house. You are welcome to smoke outside on the front porch or in the yard. Please dispose of all cigarettes in a responsible manner.

-No parties (we utilize Minut sensors that alert us when the decibel levels rise above acceptable levels for neighbors) - we WILL evict guests who violate this rule.

-If bringing pets, please ensure that they do not eliminate inside of the house or destroy any of the contents in the house. We understand that in some cases, accidents do happen. Please notify us if there are any areas of the house that an accident has occurred in. You will find a doggie care basket in the kitchen. Pets must be crated if left alone by the owner. You are more than welcome to take your pets out on a leash into the large yard. This is a shared space, so please treat it as such.

You will find the house manual on the table by the front door. It has additional info on the area, including dining recommendations and activities to consider. If you have any questions or concerns, please do not hesitate to contact us!

Arrival details—Because the code to the keyless entry door lock changes with each guest, I add the following to the *Check-in instructions*: *Guests are emailed the day of their arrival with check-in instructions and their own personal access code.*

Wi-Fi details are updated here as well.

As you may have noticed, certain key pieces of information can be found in multiple places. The more places you have the information/rules/etc., the better. It is better to repeat yourself than not to be heard the first time.

Co-Hosts

If you decide you want someone to co-host with you, here is the place to make that happen. I have my husband listed, and he can respond to guests the same as me.

Wow, well, that was a heck of a chapter! But we are finally done with it, and your listing with Airbnb should now be live and ready to go. Now you can post your property on VRBO, Booking.com, TripAdvisor and more!

Take your time, dig into the nitty-gritty details, and don't forget to *sync your calendars*!

In the next chapter, we will talk about accepting and welcoming your first guests!

Accepting and Welcoming Your First Guests

———

A s with the last two chapters, most of this is going to use the predominant online booking platform everyone is so well-versed with, Airbnb, along with its accompanying lingo. Once you clearly understand one platform, you can branch out to others and puzzle your way through them easier.

Accepting Your First Booking

Booking Inquiry vs. Booking Request—A *booking inquiry* is when a guest has a question ("Is there off-street parking that can accommodate a moving truck?" would be an example of one I have received). You, as the host, then have the option to Pre-Approve, Decline, or Respond to the inquiry.

A *booking request* is where the guest is ready to book your place, has submitted all the details (dates, number of guests, payment info, etc) and is waiting for the host to approve the reservation. A host then has the option to either Approve, Decline, or Respond.

Response Time—How quickly you as a host respond to inquiries and requests is monitored by Airbnb and other hosting platforms. Except for middle of the night communication, I try to keep my response time to within a few minutes of the initial contact. This also feeds into your future status as a Superhost, which we will discuss in Part V. I have set my notifications on my phone to let me know when there are any messages through the app. That makes it easy for me to respond in a timely manner.

Before accepting a reservation request—Before you press Accept on that first request, I strongly recommend you read Part VIII: Beware, Scammers Ahead! It will give a rundown of whom to avoid. Locals, bots, and scammers will target listings with few or no reviews. They know you are new and they are banking on you, not knowing your way around the platform yet. Whether it is a local looking to party, or a scammer who wants to pay, "my company will send you a certified check" - a newbie host is exactly who they are looking for. Proceed with caution!

Accepting your first guests—You have done your due diligence, the guest appears to be legitimate, and it is time to press the Accept button. Before you do, you should also have your Automated Messages set up and in place. Make sure you have read *Part V: Communicate Clearly and Effectively* and created your three standard messages. These messages (Reservation Confirmation, Pre-Arrival Info, and Pre-Departure Info) should have all the information a guest needs: 1) to know when they are staying at your STR (along with arrival and departure window) and what your basic rules are (no parties!), 2) the specific address and access info on the day of the reservation, and 3) when they need to leave and what (if any) expectations you have for them before leaving the STR (take out trash, wash dishes, strip beds, etc). I will strongly recommend that, no matter the nightly cost (and cleaning fees) you charge in your STR, you keep a guest's "to-do" list to the bare minimum. They aren't your children, and they don't need (or want) a chores list. And frankly, the less they have to do, the happier they will be. Happy guest = excellent review!

Welcoming Your First Guests

Self check-in vs. meet and greet—Do you allow your guests self check-in or are you there to meet and greet? For me, the answer is simple—self check-in, please! I highly recommend self check-in for a few of reasons: 1) coordinating arrival meet/greet times can be a real inconvenience to both the host and the guest (traffic, delayed flights, weather, etc.), 2) privacy and autonomy—the place feels less host-centric and more guest-centric, 3) introverts usually hate meet and greets.

Look at this way. According to the Myers-Briggs type indicator sample, 50.7% of Americans are introverts. I describe myself as a high-functioning introvert, because I can take a significant amount of exposure to others before wanting to go hide away from the world, but even I want to be left the heck alone to check in by myself to a rental space. I'm a big girl, so if I have trouble accessing the space, I'll reach out. Otherwise, leave me be. Allowing your guests to check in on their own, yet being available should they have trouble, is the happiest medium I have found.

Checking in mid-stay—If you have a guest who is staying for a week, it is a great idea to check in with them on the second or third day of their stay. I usually do this by messaging them through the online booking platform they are using. I usually say something like this:

"Hi Mary! I just wanted to check in and see if your stay is going well and you have everything you need. Let me know if there is anything I can do to make your stay more pleasant or if you need any recommendations for dining or activities. I'm happy to help!"

Other than that, you are golden. Congratulations, you have hosted your first guests!

Part V: Become the Host with the Most

———

Be a Professional

If you are thinking "I'll rent out a room in my house and make a killing!"—it's normal, I thought that way as well. But if you think that there isn't work involved, or a professional attitude that goes with this business, think again.

In fact, don't think like a homeowner, think like a business. Because that is what you are if you go into short-term rentals. You are also in the *hospitality* business. And that means being hospitable. Your job is to provide a fantastic stay to your customers. So put yourself in their shoes and imagine you are the guest. What do you want when traveling? What do you expect?

Take a moment and jot down some of those thoughts. What do YOU want from a place you are staying in? Often, I see hosts get wrapped up in weeds, the minutiae of what we do, or what a particular guest does or says, instead of looking at the bigger picture. And the bigger picture is that we must be professionals in everything we say or do. By all means, be down to earth, welcoming, humorous and even odd. I am. It's allowed. I'm plenty weird and most of my guests love that about me. But remember what is happening here. As a host, I'm providing a safe, comfortable, appealing place for someone to stay in. I want my guests to feel cared for, appreciated, and, above all, to have their basic needs met. The hospitality business is all about that. In return, I get paid. Money lands in my hand (or bank account) and I clean up, turn around, and welcome the next guest, and the next, and the next.

So what do I mean by "be a professional"? Well, be a professional...

In Presentation

Tip: Create a guest handbook or, better yet, purchase a ready-made template like this one:

https://www.etsy.com/listing/1230862426

Given enough time and energy, I could have re-created this template myself. But honestly, I would far more prefer to spend time on other things. And for the low purchase price of $5.99, it was easy to create and print off and it looks fantastic! Be sure to include a photograph of your welcome book in your listing. It shows that you are a professional host who anticipates your guests' every need!

Learn at Every Opportunity

Pop quiz. When a guest sends you a note apologizing for taking one of the charging cords provided accidentally while packing up, what do you do/say?

When this happened in early 2022, I sent back a reply thanking them for letting me know, told them to not worry about it, and put a note on my Alexa list to "Label all the charging cords."

The cord is gone, but I have extras. I'll take another cord over. The guest gets a freebie (and already loved our place so he will be back), and I've learned a very simple lesson—label everything.

As if I didn't know that already, right? Everything is a learning opportunity. When a guest suggested I consider non-slip mats in the bathtub, I bought them right away. I had to get special ones since we have an old claw-foot tub that has been resurfaced (suction cups void the warranty), but you can believe I did it right away!

Each guest suggestion, whether or not I act on it, is treated with respect and careful consideration. I want the best place for my guests; because that engenders repeat business and great reviews. And also, because it is the right thing to do.

When early on we received a few noise complaints (*from* the guests, not *about* the guests), I realized ear-plugs were in order. I ordered a gigantic bag of them and guests have mentioned them in reviews repeatedly. Folks love them!

I ask for suggestions on how we can improve the place to be posted in the private feedback section. In January 2022, we received the following suggestion:

Ray's private feedback for you:

"Melissa and I really appreciate a great place to stay for our little trip to KC. You guys definitely made the trip better. I thought I would add one thing that I thought of that would make it a little more comfy! It might be a good idea to replace the front door or find a way to seal it better. This is probably only a problem in the winter, but that front room was quite a bit colder than the rest of the house. When we had the bedroom door closed, the heat wasn't circulating, so that room was barely at 71, and bedroom 1 was at 77. Just an idea to look into, we had warm clothes, so it wasn't a problem!"

It was the first truly frigid few days of winter, and yes, I have THREE blankets and throws scattered about the living room, but Ray's suggestion is good. Instead of a new door, since it is an antique bevel glass door and very heavy and sturdy, I will probably look into a nice storm door, which would be an excellent thing to have, anyway. In warmer weather, folks hang out on the front porch or go in and out of the front door more often. A storm door that has a screen insert would keep the flying insects out in the warm months, and help conserve heat in the winter.

I don't take every guest suggestion. There have been a couple of guests who have suggested the double gate be automated, which would have cost thousands of dollars to install. My property simply doesn't earn that kind of money. I love getting this kind of feedback. It gives me a plan for the future as I continue to craft the best guest experience possible.

I urge you to keep an open mind when you receive reviews. You don't need to offer discounts or comp someone's stay for the tiniest thing wrong, and you don't need to cater to their every whim, but many of my guest's suggestions, questions, or issues have taught me more than any book I read or podcast I listened to when preparing to open my first short-term rental.

I'll go into detail on reviews in Part VI. Another vital aspect of being a professional STR host is communicating professionally. So much so that I dedicated this next chapter to that. Read on...

Communicate Clearly and Effectively

So much of truly great hospitality boils down to communication. Are we conveying our expectations to our guests clearly? Are we responsive to their needs? Have we been clear in our instructions for check-in, for the various idiosyncrasies of the property they are staying in, and for their eventual check out? No matter how clear we are, there will be guests who ignore or don't notice details, so it is important to walk the line between over-delivering (and annoying them) to under-delivering (and getting annoyed ourselves when they don't follow our guidelines or requests).

I try to over-deliver. I state our rules and other helpful information in the listings online, in the guidebook inside of each STR, and through signs scattered in relevant locations throughout the property. If this seems like over-kill, keep this in mind; your guests are often traveling on the road all day and looking for a place to crash. They are exhausted, their hands full of pets, kids, and they have full lives we know nothing about. They may be traveling to see family, undergo a medical procedure, or deal with the death of a loved one. A thousand other things might tug at their attention from when they 1) make the reservation, 2) finally arrive, or 3) are in the middle of their stay. Our job is to convey the information in as succinct a manner as possible and then step out of their way so they can enjoy their stay.

Communicating with guests takes finesse. For me, as an author and lifelong reader and writer, writing is something I do every day. I also spent over twenty years in a variety of corporate settings, and that taught me volumes about proper business communication. That said, I have a great deal of experience to share with you. I will include plenty of examples.

There is a fine line between too much communication and too little. There is also your "voice," which hopefully will be warm and welcoming but also business appropriate.

Let's start with these general tips:

- Make a Connection with Your Guests

- Wording, it's all in the wording

- Create templates and auto-messages

We are going to tackle each of these later in this chapter. Having a line of clear, professional communication at all times will save you thousands of dollars in lost fees, damages, and the middle of the night "I can't access the space" messages.

Make a Connection with Your Guests

We crave human connection. Even for myself, as an introvert, this holds true. When you create a positive connection with another human being, you help them see you as a human being worthy of kindness and appreciation. You are no longer a faceless financial transaction.

So how do we do this? How do we create a connection while continuing to hold fast on good business principles?

This can and will vary, but I'll give you some examples later. Check them out under *Part VIII: A Multitude of Tips* and then think about how you can incorporate your own personality and create a connection with your guests...

About Us—In each of the STRs I create, I put in an *About Us* write-up, usually framed and set on the entry desk. It talks about how my husband and I met in high school in the mid-'80s but never dated, not until 20 years later. How we finished raising my teen daughter and then had another baby, then became foster parents of three, and eventually being lucky enough to adopt two of our littles. It talks about us buying the property we have now and turning it into an oasis of greenery, with a pond, fruit trees, and more. This creates a human connection, a personal one. It says, in no uncertain terms, that we are people who live and love. Parents who love their kids and each other and the land they are on. And that can be a powerful connection. Also, if you make yourself likable, it's harder for folks to eviscerate you in a review when things go awry.

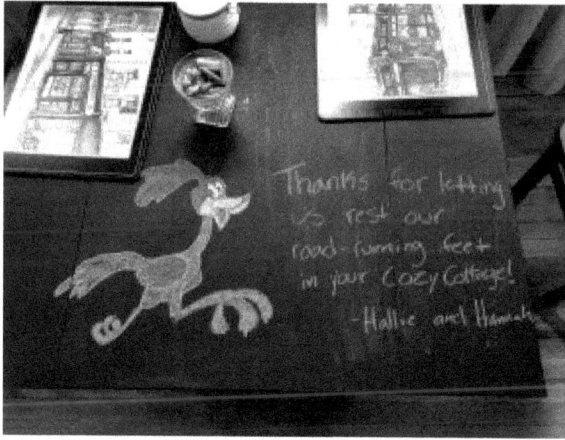

Art of The Cottages—It all started with the finish wearing out on the kitchen table. We have a table in Cottage West's kitchen that can seat four people. It was a dark finish, almost black, and around six months after we opened for business, I noticed that the finish was wearing off in some spots. Worse, it simply looked... dirty. A huge no-no in the hospitality business. I painted the top of it with chalkboard paint until we could afford to buy a new one. And when the paint was dry, I grabbed a couple of pieces of chalk and wrote "Welcome to Cottage West!" on the table.

With each guest, I would re-do the welcome note. Soon enough, the art started showing up. I ended up stocking the house with a variety of chalk colors and things just took off from there. When we rolled out the Hedy Lamarr Airstream, I was determined to replicate the fun and finished the top of the dinette table with several coats of chalkboard paint.

I find the *coolest* art left behind by our guests! Absolutely beautiful designs, and I began posting pictures of it on The Cottages Facebook page and also my Instagram account. A friend suggested The Cottages needed their own Instagram account, and I created @TheCottagesArt where I am seeing a decent following.

I also printed out the photos and added them to photo albums which are in all of my short-term rentals, along with "the story of" for each of our rentals (cross-pollinating guests from one rental to another).

The Story Of—The most powerful connection of all is the story of how we purchased Cottage West and renovated her. We have a binder full of photos of our "$25 House" and what we did to return her from a crumbling, unloved ruin into a warm, welcoming short-term rental. My mother once told me, "Don't tell anyone you bought the house for $25." When I asked why, she sniffed and said, "They'll think you are a slumlord."

The exact opposite is true. First, people cannot believe I actually bought a house for $25. As I recount the story and show pictures of the renovation process, they understand just how massive the project was for us, especially for two first-time home renovators. Our love for our community shines through. We live in this neighborhood, on the same street as our short-term rentals. We rescued a house that sat unloved and crumbling for over a decade and returned it to a functioning home that brings new people into our area and gives them a great sense of who we are and the community we hope to create.

I can't tell you how many people love reading the story of Cottage West. We receive so many comments on it, all positive, and I think it feeds our natural human curiosity about other places and things. Think of Paul Harvey's long-running radio show where he would tell "The Rest of the Story" or The Moth Radio Hour (a podcast that I listen to regularly).

Inside of the binder, we have included what scant history of the house and neighborhood we know. We have found objects during the renovation—Civil War bayonets, Depression-era glassware, a Civil War uniform button, a ring made from a bent spoon, and so much more. We included newspaper clippings, one from 1929 when a fire nearly gutted the house, and the old 1940 tax photo. Doing so, recognizing the generations before us, really engages our guests.

In August 2021, my husband and I scheduled a mini-vacation to Austin, Texas, and stayed in a fantastic old Airstream Airbnb. Inside of it, the owner had her own "story of" that detailed her buying the property, becoming a foster and adoptive mom, and creating a haven for her children and her guests. I loved it! She branded it "the home that love built" and I couldn't have agreed more. Next to that, she had journal upon journal of notes from guests who had stayed. I wrote my entry, feeling as if I were a part of her story.

No need to read minds, conduct a poll—I recently added a poll to Cottage West. We provide Netflix, Hulu, Curiosity Stream, and Amazon Prime. I wanted to see if I should change that configuration and add more or less to our streaming service offerings. So, I created a poll. This serves two purposes, really. For one, it allows me to collect opinions and get meaningful data on what folks are watching. For two, it shows a willingness on my part, their host, to provide them with the entertainment *they* want. Yet another indicator of hospitality.

Wording, It's All in the Wording

How can you communicate effectively and positively with a guest? It is all in the wording. Keep in mind that text can leave room for misinterpretation, or attitude, so here are a few things to keep in mind:

- Use proper spelling, punctuation and grammar

- Avoid the word "NO" as much as possible.

- Point out the positives

- Stay professional

- Have boundaries (and stick to them)

How would you handle the following questions and situations listed below?

Can You Stock Milk?—A potential guest reached out and asked...

"I see you list the kitchen as fully stocked. I'm a big milk drinker. Will you stock plenty of milk for me?"

Whew, let's unpack that for a moment. A milk drinker. Okay. Is that cow's milk? Oat milk? Almond? Soy? Whole milk? Skim? Something in between? How much do you consider plenty? A quart? A gallon? What?

I wrote back,

"We provide basic cooking supplies (flour, sugar, coffee, spices) - anything that is non-perishable. However, I am happy to direct you to several grocery stores that are just a few minutes' drive away."

No, I didn't get that booking and honestly; I was relieved. What else would this person have asked for while staying with me?

My Brother is Allergic to Something in Your Apartment, Can We Get a Refund?

158

This was a situation posted on one of the host support groups on Facebook. I was very impressed with how the host responded, though. Here is the conversation:

Guest: My brother's allergies are triggering and he is getting sick from something in the apartment. Will it be possible for us to get a refund?

Host: I'm sorry your brother has allergies. What is he allergic to? When a guest tells us beforehand, we can see if it is possible to accommodate. We've had guests with allergies to certain cleaning products and we avoided using them prior to their stay. Depending on what the allergy is, we can see if we can remove it. We can also schedule a cleaner to go over and clean everything again. (This can be coordinated and would be billed at the rate of our current cleaning fee) Currently, we use natural products like vinegar or Castile soap. We also have always had a strict no pets policy as I have severe pet allergies.

Please let me know what your travel insurance needs. I hate you will miss out on staying with us! If you didn't purchase travel insurance, the best I can offer is a partial refund should I be able to book the remaining days of your stay. Once you cancel, it will open up the calendar to allow another guest to book. I will only be able to refund what they book for. Thank you in advance for your understanding.

I really loved their response. It was thoughtful, covered all the bases—from CYA (cover your ass) to addressing any potential arguments the guest might raise and even reminding them of why travelers should purchase traveler's insurance—and did it in a polite and kind manner. It models one host's way of showing empathy while still keeping a head for business and their bottom line.

Will Your Fence Keep a Fence-Jumping Dog In? - I will admit, I laughed when I saw this question. As I've previously discussed, our properties allow dogs, but we expect the guests to be responsible pet owners and keep their pets leashed when outside and keeping the inside mess and damage-free.

This potential guest didn't tell me exactly how large their pet was, but it didn't really matter because if they were asking how tall the fence was, they hadn't realized that: 1) the yard is shared with our house (even though it clearly states it in the listing), or 2) they fully intended to let their pet run loose through the yard. I'm sorry, but when you are traveling with your pet, it's simply good behavior to have them leashed unless told otherwise. I responded kindly, but firmly, sticking to my listed rules...

"Hi Anna! Thank you for your interest. Our fences are only 4 1/2 feet tall, but this is a shared yard and we require all pets to be leashed for our and other guests' comfort and safety."

No, she didn't book, and I was absolutely fine with that.

Can We Get a Discount?—A previous guest reached out to ask if he could get a discount on an upcoming stay. He noted that my prices had gone up and wanted to know if there was any wiggle room on that. Now, as I've already likely mentioned, and as you will see in my financial spreadsheets in a later chapter, my prices are rather competitive and often far lower than a certain neighborhood just to the north of me. I know that my particular neighborhood is not the best (although it is far from the worst) and that I'm targeting a particular guest—one who is looking for a reasonably low price. Yes, penny pinchers. I'm one myself, so I know my kind pretty darn well!

The idea of discounting my properties further than I already have is not attractive to me. He had stayed before and he could have signed up for my newsletter (the signs are everywhere providing a link). If he had done that, he could have easily contacted me directly and I would have provided him a direct booking rate that, while cheaper for him, actually makes me more money than going through one of the hosting platforms. But he hadn't, and I have no way of pointing him to that through Airbnb's messaging platform without violating their terms of service.

Instead, I wrote...

"Hi Marc! We have another Airbnb that is available at a lower price overall, if you are interested. We just brought it online in late spring. It's a lot of fun, and in the same location. Here is the link in case you are interested [link to Hedy Lamarr Airstream]."

You notice I didn't say no to him. I simply directed him to a slightly cheaper alternative. If you don't have a second property to cross-promote, no worries! My backup options were...

"Hi Marc! Cottage West is already discounted by [$20] below the going rate. Let me know if you are interested in booking; we would love to have you back!"

OR...

"Hi Marc! Thank you so much for thinking of us! Yes, unfortunately, costs have gone up regarding cleaning fees. We pay our cleaners a living wage. After all, they work very hard! Let me know if you would like to book; we would love to have you back."

I didn't say no. But I also made it clear I would not cave. Two days after, Marc sent the inquiry. He came back and said...

"Hey Christine! Thanks for sending the alternate option. Unfortunately, I don't think it will be big enough for our dog, Figgy. But it's not looking like there is much else in the area for the price you offer, so we might just try to make it work with the cottage!"

Why? Because reality interceded. We over-deliver in amenities and accommodations. No one else is going to let them stay for less AND allow pets. Not for the price point that I have listed.

My point in all of this is to suggest that you stick to your stated fees while over-delivering all the way. This is why Cottage West stays over 90% booked on average. The price is right; the reviews are stellar, and I over-deliver on quality for the price.

Can we change the reservation dates? – Guests occasionally have last-minute changes and recently I received a trip alteration request. The guest was due in four days, and was requesting to move their reservation to six weeks away. Now, occasionally a savvy Airbnb guest asks for an alteration request like this in order to circumvent your cancellation policy. For example, canceling just four days before with my moderate cancellation policy means that a guest is entitled to a refund on cleaning fees only. If they were to reschedule to a date outside of the cancellation policy (seven days or more) they could then receive a full refund. Some folks tend to abuse it, so I offer last-minute cancellations this little bone...

Hi Susan! I'm so sorry your plans have changed. I was looking forward to hosting you! In cases like this, where a guest has a last-minute change to their travel plans, I ask that you cancel your reservation. If I receive a booking from a guest in your place (definitely possible due to our central local) then I will reimburse any funds I would have received for your reservation.

Guests tend to understand my reasoning. After all, they knew when booking what kind of cancellation policy I have and agreed to it, and my offer goes above and beyond that policy. I don't have to offer it, and in fact I don't unless they come to me and ask for it. A guest typically cancels and then I put a note in my calendar to send them a refund if and when another guest books in their place.

Why so much? - Occasionally, you may alter your pricing down in order to fill a vacancy. I actually do this a lot in the off-season and on weekdays versus weekends. My pricing on Cottage West can fall as low as $60 per night. When it does, I've received messages questioning why the total price is nearly double that, since it includes a cleaning fee and fees that Airbnb charges.

Here's a great way to respond to a potential guest questioning why the fee of $60 per night doubled...

"Hi Rhiauna! Thank you for your interest in Cottage West! You are actually renting Cottage West with a deeply discounted nightly fee of $62, instead of the normal $85 weekday night or $105 weekend price. The cleaning fee that accompanies it does not change because our loyal cleaners get paid a fair wage. The rest are fees that Airbnb charges guests. We hope you will decide to stay with us!"

This doesn't always work, but it gives the guest a point of reference. They are looking at a property that normally rents for as much as $105 per night, and the cleaning fee has remained the same because the hosts care about their cleaners. That's the message you want to give them—that $62 is a *deep* nightly discount. It isn't the standard price at all. If they are uninterested, then it is likely that they cannot afford it anyway and would be better staying at a budget motel.

Create Templates and Auto Messages

Let's dive into some messages you can prepare and, with Airbnb, auto-schedule so you never have to worry about forgetting to send a message again. As I'll probably mention ad nauseum, over 90% of my income comes from Airbnb. You will hear me use a lot of examples from Airbnb, and it is because, of all the platforms, they have the most streamlined and advanced systems in place. And with the three most important messages, Airbnb even has an option to make them automated, which is a lifesaver if you are busy with another job, or family, or just plain busy all the way around like I am.

In this section, I will include examples of all of my automated messages. I encourage you to copy them, edit them for your own needs, and use them. I've managed to weed out all the issues/mistakes. You will too. Everything is a learning curve. But let's get on to the three messages. And yes, I have these all set up as automated, scheduled messages in Airbnb. I also have them set up as templates on VRBO. When I get the occasional guest on Booking.com, or a direct booking, I copy and paste, and if necessary, edit, my Airbnb message to fit. Here I am using my messages to a guest named Conner as an example:

CHRISTINE D. SHUCK

Christine 4:11 PM

Hi Bonnar! Thank you for reserving Cottage West - Central Locale Close & Convenient.

This is an automated message sent upon confirmation of reservation. Let me know if you have any questions, I'm here to help!

Thank you for reserving Cottage West, I am sure you will enjoy your stay at this warm and welcoming space! Just to confirm, I have you down to check in anytime after 2pm on: Sep 18, 2022 and to check out by 11am on Sep 19, 2022.

The morning of your arrival, I will send you the address, detailed instructions on accessing the space, as well as our direct contact info. We are usually available to meet you if you would wish, but you are more than welcome to check yourself in.

I'm just down the street (the large brick house with wraparound porch at the opposite end of the large, shared yard) and ready to assist should you need anything.

Please also let me know if you need any suggestions on great dining, shopping, or other fun adventures. There are plenty suggested in the guest handbook inside of Cottage West, but we can direct you to local breweries and other great destinations.

Thanks again and we look forward to hosting you!

Confirmation—Sent automatically immediately after they place a reservation. This message basically says:

- Name of guest

- Dates of stay (including check-in time)

- Thanks for booking and I'll reach out on the day of your arrival with further info

- Let me know if you need any dining/shopping/activity suggestions

I put in a little more. Like the fact that I'm just down the street. That there is a shared yard (also listed in the listing). Occasionally a person looking to party slips through, sees this and knows the chances are they will be shut down quickly with hosts so close and they cancel right away. Believe me, I would far prefer a cancellation to getting some mess of a party on my quiet street and irritating my neighbors.

It's short, friendly, and to the point. The Pre-Arrival message is significantly longer.

Good Morning Conner!

This an automated message that will give you all the details you need to access Cottage West. I will respond as quickly as possible to any direct messages you send through the app.

Thank you for choosing to stay at Cottage West! Here is the information you need to access the property for your stay:

COTTAGE WEST ADDRESS: ▓▓▓▓▓▓▓▓▓▓▓▓▓▓▓

CROSS STREETS ▓▓▓▓▓▓▓▓▓

CHECK IN: Anytime after 2pm. If you need something sooner, please let me know and I'll do my best to accommodate.

PARKING: Off street, gated parking is available to all Cottage West guests. Please park on the right hand side of the gravel driveway inside of the double gates and then close the gates behind you. The left hand side of the driveway is for our Airstream Airbnb guests, so please do not park there.

ACCESS: Type ▓▓▓▓ into the keypad at the front door and press the Kwikset button at the top once. Occasionally it sticks, pull it firmly towards you and try again. The door will lock automatically within 30 seconds so please make sure you memorize the code or have your phone with access instructions nearby. Please be sure to press the Kwikset button at the top to lock it when leaving the house.

ALARM: The house also has a security alarm with motion sensors. You will find the security alarm panel on the wall of the living room, almost directly in front of you as you come in through the door. Enter ▓▓ to disarm only IF it is going off (we don't typically set it). If you wish to engage the alarm when inside, click on "Arm Stay" or if leaving "Arm Away" and enter the code.

OUR HOME (NOT Cottage West): We live at ▓▓▓▓▓▓ It's the big brick house directly to the east. We share the large yard with Cottage West. Our dogs use a separate, dedicated yard.

CONTACT INFO: If you have any questions, please do not hesitate to contact us through the platform or call/text me at ▓▓▓▓▓▓. My husband's name is Dave and his cell phone # is ▓▓▓▓▓▓.

NO PARTIES and NO SMOKING INDOORS: As a reminder, we do not allow parties or loud events at Cottage West. Our property is equipped with a Minut sensor that will notify us of loud noises. We have many families with young children (including our own family) living on our street and believe in respecting the rights of our neighbors. We also do not allow smoking or vaping of any kind inside of Cottage West and will assess a $100 additional cleaning fee to violators (the property includes a FreshAir sensor technology that will alert us to tobacco or marijuana smoke). Please keep any and all smoking outside. Thank you in advance for honoring our rules.

PETS: If you have any pets, please keep them leashed in the yard as it is a shared space for us, and for the Airstream guests who may also have pets. Thank you!

Pre-Arrival—At 5 a.m. the day of their arrival, my second message goes out. This is the longest of the three messages and contains the most important information. It includes:

- Address of property

- Cross streets

- Check-in time (for the second time, in case they have forgotten).

- Parking instructions

- Access instructions

- Our home address (this is unnecessary, but I like to share it again, just in case folks didn't get the message the first time that we live right next door to our Airbnb)

- Contact info (yes, we encourage on-platform communication, but we aren't always home when they arrive or we might be asleep, so it helps to have some kind of way for them to contact us)

- Reminder of rules (no parties, no smoking indoors)

- Pet policy (we allow pets, but we have a few rules about them)

It's long. I won't lie. But there is a certain level of CYA here (cover your ass) that needs to be done so that Airbnb, or whatever platform you are on, knows you have communicated effectively with your guests and given them every piece of information that they need.

Finally, we have a third auto-message that goes out.

> **Christine** 5:07 AM
> Good Morning Conner!
>
> This is an automated message sent the morning of checkout.
>
> Checkout is at 11:00 a.m. If you end up leaving earlier, please let me know so that we can arrange for the cleaners to come. Thank you for staying at Cottage West, I hope that your stay was peaceful and comfortable.
>
> Any used bath or kitchen linens can be set in the laundry basket in the hallway. There is no need to strip any used bed linens, we will handle that. Please do not re-make any beds used. And if you could please wash any used dishes, that would be fantastic! If you are in a hurry, don't worry about it at all.
>
> There is no need to set the alarm. We have been noticing difficulties with the auto-lock feature lately, so just press the Kwikset button at the top to lock it when you leave the house.
>
> We would love for you to join our monthly newsletter. You will see the link to that in the note inside the property regarding saving money on future bookings.
>
> We hope you have had a 5 star stay, please don't forget to review. We are also very open to private comments on how we can improve the space for your return visit in the future.
>
> Thanks again and safe travels!

Pre-Departure—Also sent at 5 a.m. the morning of checkout. It is relatively quick and to the point.

- Check-out time

- Basic instructions—put used linens in the laundry basket, wash your dirty dishes (they don't always do it and I don't sweat it; that's what I have a cleaning fee for)

- Wording that encourages them to leave a 5-star review and to direct any comments on how we can improve to the private comments section (instead of the main review).

- Thank them for staying with us and wish them safe travels

A debate on one of the host Facebook groups recently arose about my timing for sending the checkout instructions. I send mine at 5 am the day of departure, and according to some remarks, that would be a horrible time to send any correspondence to a guest who was on vacation. Fair enough. But 99% of my guests are one-night stays. Some come to visit the city, but most are driving through. If I send the checkout message the evening before, I'm often sending it before they have ever arrived, which feels weird to me, and would likely be very confusing to the road weary traveler! If I wait until a later hour, I get messages from the guests saying they have already checked out. The time I send the checkout instructions works for me and my guests, but not necessarily for others. Assess your guests. How long do they typically stay for? What is their reason for staying at your STR? Obviously, these are questions you won't be able to answer until you have hosted quite a few. Until that time, you may wish to prepare the checkout template, and send it out manually until you have a solid feel for who your average guests are and what they expect.

Attaining Superhost Status

———

As soon as you begin hosting, it is important to achieve the Superhost status as soon as possible. It is relatively easy to attain and carries with it some significant benefits. I was lucky enough to attain Superhost status after three months of having Cottage West available as my first STR back in January 2020 and have maintained that status ever since. As of mid-October 2022, I have accumulated over 573 reviews and a 4.9-star rating on Airbnb for our two STR properties. Below, you will learn more about why it is important, how to qualify, and more.

Why It's Important

- *Earn extra money*—Superhosts often benefit from a significant increase in earnings. More visibility and trust from guests can mean more money for you.

- *Attract more guests*—The badge can make your listing more attractive to guests—they'll know you're an experienced host known for great hospitality. Guests can even filter their search results to discover only listings with the Superhost status.

- *Gain access to exclusive rewards*—You'll get an extra 20% on top of the usual bonus when you refer new hosts. After four consecutive quarters as a Superhost, you'll receive a travel coupon. (I've received two "$100 off an Airbnb stay" coupons so far!). In case you haven't taken advantage of it yet, earn $40 from Airbnb by using my host referral link to start hosting now! www.airbnb.com/r/strsuccess[1] *Note: This is zero cost to you. I do not receive any percentage of your income. Airbnb is simply paying me a finder's fee for referring you to them.*

What Are the Qualifications?

---
1. http://www.airbnb.com/r/strsuccess

In order to qualify for Superhost status on Airbnb, you need four must-haves. You must:

1. *Maintain a high overall rating*—You must have a 4.8 or higher average overall rating based on reviews from your Airbnb guests in the past year. Guests know they can expect outstanding hospitality from these hosts.
2. *Be experienced*—You must have hosted at least 10 stays in the past year, or if you host longer-term reservations, 100 nights over at least 3 stays. Guests can feel confident staying with an experienced host.
3. *Avoid cancellations*—You must have canceled less than 1% of the time, not including extenuating circumstances. * This means zero cancellations if you have fewer than 100 reservations in a year. Rare cancellations mean more peace of mind for guests.
4. *Be responsive*—You must have responded to 90% of new, booking-related messages within 24 hours. When guests ask you questions, they know they'll get a quick reply.

* Extenuating circumstances include: changes to government travel requirements, declared emergencies or epidemics, government travel restrictions, military actions and other hostilities, and natural disasters. You can learn more about Airbnb's extenuating circumstances policy here:

https://www.airbnb.com/help/article/1320/extenuating-circumstances-policy

Four times a year, you'll have the chance to qualify for Superhost status. Airbnb checks all hosts every three months based on their previous 365 days of hosting. If hosts have areas to improve, they need to meet all requirements by the next assessment to earn or keep their Superhost status. I've maintained a Superhost status since I first qualified for it in January 2020.

A Word to the Wise

I've just talked about how being a Superhost can be important, right? Well, now, forget all that. Don't obsess over it. Don't worry about it. Yes, it has its benefits, but it is certainly not the be-all and end-all. Even more so, don't allow your fears of not getting, or losing, that status once you have it, stop you from enforcing your basic rules with guests. I hate seeing hosts worry about their "perfect 5-star track record" or stress over a manipulative guest who threatens the newly minted Superhost status of a new host. You *will* get a less-than-stellar review in your hosting career and for another thing, concentrate on the guests you have coming in, *not* on those you can no longer do anything about.

Part VI: Cleaning, Dealing with Reviews, Solving Problems

Cleaning Your STR - Step-by-Step

— —

I ran a cleaning business for fifteen years—from 2005 until early 2020. Until COVID came around and shook my little tree hard, I had around a dozen regular clients that I cleaned regularly. Several had been with me for all fifteen of those years. Except around two years when I took time off to have my second child, all the cleanings were handled by me personally. I specialized in residential cleanings and customized each cleaning to my clients' unique needs. I handled deep cleanings and regular maintenance cleanings. So when I say that I know how to clean a property, you know I have the experience and capacity.

You may not be interested in cleaning your STR and I totally get that. But I would ask you to consider doing it, if you have the time and the ability, for at least a few turnovers, before handing it off to someone else. I suggest this for several reasons:

1. It gives you an idea of just how long it takes to clean your STR property.
2. It is an excellent skill to have in a pinch. There will be issues with cleaners (losing a cleaner, having to hire another), and knowing what needs to be done can really help.
3. It allows you to keep good tabs on your property. You will notice issues better than anyone else.
4. It can save you a lot of money (approximately 40% of my total earnings would go to cleaners if I didn't clean the property myself).

Honestly, I make good money for a few minutes of work. And with my STRs just steps away from me, it makes financial sense since I am working from home. This might not be the same situation for you, and I understand. I can clean Cottage West in 45 minutes and the Hedy Lamarr Airstream takes me around 15 minutes. And considering I'm earning $50-$65 in cleaning fees for Cottage West, and $25 for the Airstream, that's a decent amount of money for right at an hour of work in a day. However, it may or may not make sense for you. If you don't end up cleaning your own STR, make sure and schedule regular check-ins so that you can maintain a high standard of care for the property. Look for dust on molding and just check the general level of cleanliness overall.

Unlike a standard residential cleaning, turning over a short-term rental is a little different. Whereas I never changed linens or washed laundry in my cleaning biz, I certainly do now! I also wash dishes as needed, and restock supplies and keep track of what I need to buy more of. However, we can still break it down into easily accomplished steps.

But first, let's talk about what cleaning supplies you need. Below is a basic list of supplies. I will admit that I have always preferred to use as few chemicals as possible. Humans seem to spray a lot of crap into the air that we don't need to be breathing, and with many guests being sensitive to scents and strong chemicals, it makes sense to keep it as green as possible. It is also better for your bottom line. Here is what you will need to clean your STR on regular turnovers and the occasional deep clean:

- High/low extendable duster with fan-blade attachment

- Microfiber cloths (washable and reusable)

- Paper towels

- Blue scrub sponges (they are non-scratch)

- Comet cleanser

- Simple Green

- Glass cleaner (or water, which is what I use)

- Vacuum

- Broom and dustpan

- Mop and bucket

- Enzyme floor cleanser

I suggest having these on hand in the STR at all times. Guests will often try to clean up if they have made a mess, and who are we to interfere with that?! I usually keep my supplies in a clearly marked cabinet in the kitchen. The bigger pieces (vacuum, mop, duster) are on a tool rack in a corner of the laundry room.

Read on—here is your step-by-step guide to cleaning (and restocking) your own short-term rental...

Regular Cleaning

Quick walk through—Before beginning your cleaning, take a moment to walk through the property. Is there anything missing, broken, or damaged? Note it and take a picture. A phone that you can take notes on is essential. I have a running "to-do" list on mine for supplies, fixes, etc.

Laundry—The absolute first thing I do *after* a quick walk-through is to gather the laundry. This is especially important if you have laundry facilities there in the property. You can pop a load into the wash and then work through the rest of the house to get it prepared for the next guest. Cottage West has a washer and dryer. I start the load washing, and by the time I'm done cleaning the house, the wash is done and ready to be put into the dryer. I actually leave the house while the load is still drying and just fold it later at the next turnover. A note in the laundry room explains this to guests, and I keep a spare laundry basket there to put the clean laundry in if they need to use the washer and dryer.

Bathroom (s)—Bathrooms are incredibly important to guests. They don't want to see smudges on the mirrors, dirt, hair, or stains of any kind. Because we are at our most vulnerable (i.e., *naked*) in bathrooms (and in bedrooms) these areas must be *pristine*.

Surfaces—Begin with wiping down all surfaces with a clean, damp microfiber towel. Look at the fronts of cabinets, especially around the handles for prints or toothpaste etc.).

CHRISTINE D. SHUCK

Mirrors—Clean the mirrors. I typically moisten a microfiber with water, then follow it up with a dry microfiber. I try to keep my chemical usage down to as low of levels as possible.

Toilet—Spray down the toilet from top to bottom (and floor as long as it isn't carpeted) with Simple Green and then wipe down with paper towels, getting all marks, hairs, etc. off of the toilet. I usually sprinkle a little Comet cleanser in the toilet bowl and scrub it out with a toilet brush (including up under the rim) before flushing it all away. Toilets should always be spotless in your STR. Seriously, this is a trigger point with guests.

Sink—Wipe down or scrub (if necessary) the sink. Make sure the drain is clear of all hair or detritus. Shine the sink hardware and wipe down any spots of toothpaste and more from hardware and wall above. Pick up any dish soaps and wipe them down, removing water spots or pools of water from any part of the sink.

Bathtub/shower—If you have hard water, consider using a tub/tile cleaner spray. I use Simple Green, spray it around our claw-foot bathtub, and scrub using a blue scrub (non-scratch) sponge. Rinse thoroughly, removing any stray hairs. Check that the drain is operating correctly, and that it isn't draining slow.

Restock—Open cabinets and check your levels. Is the shower stocked with shampoo, conditioner, and body wash? Is there a full bottle of hand soap on the sink? Do you have enough toilet paper? I keep at least four rolls on hand in the bathroom and another eight or more in the supply cabinet in the hallway outside the bathroom. We also stock a variety of analgesics (generic Excedrin, Tylenol, and Advil) by the two-tablet packet (three packets of each), along with Q-Tips, individually wrapped toothbrushes, toothpaste, sore throat lozenges, flossers, cotton balls, and plenty more. I've set it up to make it easy to check their numbers and restock as needed. More on that later.

Kitchen—Wipe down all surfaces—not just for crumbs but also for dust.

Small and large appliances—Wipe down the insides of small appliances (microwave, toaster oven, etc.) and the outsides as well. Look for fingerprints, food particles, stains, and eradicate them.

Sink—Rinse out the sink, or give it a good scrub if needed. I suggest a blue scrub sponge and Comet.

Table and chairs—Wipe down the table and chairs, including under the edges of the table, salt and pepper shakers, etc.

Dishes—Give the dishes and glasses a once-over. Even when you have a dishwasher, things can stay on your dishes, like lipstick on a wine glass, for example. Make sure everything is sparkling clean or re-do it if necessary.

Refrigerator—Check the inside of the fridge and freezer for food and more. I recently found glass shards in a freezer. Yikes! I'm guessing a guest was trying to cool down a drink, and it didn't end well. Wipe away any food or dirt from the shelves. *A note on condiments: I put in a fair number of condiments when I started Cottage West and along the way other guests have added their own. I leave them there. As long as they aren't past their expiration date or show any signs of spoilage, I leave them there for other guests to use.* Anything like milk or leftovers, I get rid of, but not the condiments.

Restock—Make sure the soaps at the sink are full and that there are plenty of napkins, a variety of sweeteners (we carry sugar, saccharine (Sweet 'n Low), sucralose (Splenda) aspartame (Equal) and stevia packets), coffee, spices and more available. I also make sure no dishes are broken or chipped and needing to be replaced.

Bedrooms—As I mentioned above with bathrooms, bedrooms should be immaculate. Your guests want to sink into bed and sleep (or do other things) with the feeling that they are safe, comfortable, and well cared for. How can you help them feel that way?

Beds—Strip the sheets from the beds and examine the sheets, blanket, and quilt/comforter/coverlet for marks. I do not wash the blankets or quilt with every turn-over, but seasonally or as needed. Make the beds, straighten any bed skirts, tuck everything in nice and neat. I usually add a tray with two towels and washcloths neatly folded, along with my two business cards (one for The Cottages and one for my author business).

Dust and tidy—Dust anything that needs dusting. Straighten items. Is everything where it is supposed to be? Clean any mirrors.

Restock—Does each bedroom have what it needs? We stock a set of earplugs on each side of every bed—include at least one Kleenex box per room—each nightstand has a coaster for setting drinks on, a notepad and pen on a nightstand, and I make sure that each bed has at least two sets of bath towels and washcloths waiting in a bed tray.

All other common spaces—Dust as needed, looking especially for hair and crumbs. Straighten wall art, books, games—organize anything that is out of place—plump couch cushions, fold any throws, and prepare the common spaces for the next guests. This is also when I water any plants (which are a bonus to any STR, as long as you have short enough stays that the plants won't die due to neglect).

Trash—Combine all the trash into the kitchen trash and remove to the outside bins. If needed, replace all smaller lined wastebaskets with new liners. I often re-use a liner (except for the kitchen trash) if it appears clean. What can I say? It saves a few dollars and reduces waste.

Vacuum and mop—I think this is pretty self-explanatory. Vacuum the entire property and then mop as needed.

Take photos—Why take photos? Evidence and insurance. If you are very lucky, you won't get any ne'er-do-wells in your STR. But if you do, and they try to claim crazy stuff that isn't true, abscond with items, or damage the interior of your property, the photos can really come in handy for submitting a claim to the booking platform or even for stopping a scam in its tracks. Take one to two photos of each room and then delete the photos after the four-week mark has elapsed.

That's basically the regular, everyday turnover in a nutshell. Really, it isn't too bad. There is also the occasional deep cleaning that should happen, which I will talk about next. I suggest doing this on anywhere between every one to three months. If you find that your property stays spotless, you can extend it to once every other month or even quarterly. No matter what, the occasional deep cleaning will keep your property in the pristine shape it should be in for your guests. It is also an excellent opportunity to note any areas that need painting, or wood that need touching up.

Let's look at what you will need to do for a deep cleaning:

Deep Cleaning

Quick walk-through—Take a moment or two to look with a critical eye for missing paint, gouges that need repair, floors, furniture, and more in need of improvement or repair. Staying on top of these will ensure your STR looks just like the pictures promise your guests that it will. And if things change, get moved around, or are replaced, be sure to take photos and upload them to Airbnb.

High/low dusting—For this, you will need an extendable duster that doubles as a fan blade duster (if you have ceiling fans). Use it to clean your fan blades off, along with the glass covers on any lights. Run the duster along the top of all walls where the wall meets the ceiling, where cobwebs like to congregate. Run the duster along the baseboards, to each corner, and under all furniture.

Molding/door frames—Take a Magic Eraser to molding and door frames. Look high and low. The low areas are often easy to miss, but if your guests have pets or small children, that's where the marks are going to be.

Windows—Clean the insides and outsides of the glass windows and examine the curtains on at least a quarterly or bi-annual basis. Wipe down the inside track where bugs and dirt congregate. If you can't schedule a down day for the property, consider having backup sets of curtains and wash them at least one to two times per year, or as needed.

<u>Couches and chairs</u>—Remove cushions and vacuum up any hair, food, etc. Examine the cushions carefully for food, stains, or damage.

<u>Insides of cabinets and closets</u>—Re-organize supplies and wipe down the insides of all the cabinets, drawers, and closets. In the kitchen, take the time to remove the silverware organizer and wash that down. Same with the dish drainer, or if you have it, the inside of the dishwasher.

<u>Take photos</u>—Have you changed anything? Moved furniture? Switched out any décor? Now is the time to take photos to update your listing.

Now that I have covered regular turnovers and deep cleanings, I hope you feel competent when cleaning your STR. However, there may be times when you need cleaners, when you need to be out of town, or when you simply don't want to do your own cleanings. I get it, I really do. Let's talk about what you need to do to hire a service.

Hiring a Service

You want to hire out the turnovers to someone capable of handling it. I completely understand! Eventually, when we have all four STRs in operation, I will be hard-pressed to keep up with all the cleanings of all of them. I will also need to hire some of the work out. Right now, I only need a cleaning service once a year, when we fly away on our week-long family vacation to the West Coast.

To date, I hired another host for one year to handle the cleanings. I returned that first year to a layer of dust throughout Cottage West, and a stray hair in the bathroom sink. I'm very particular about cleanliness with my STRs, and that just didn't work for me. The next year, I hired a friend known for her obsessive cleanliness. My friend was just the exacting level of clean I needed.

I hope that I have properly described how clean a property needs to be and how important it is to your livelihood and future bookings to ensure it is up to a guest's expectations. Because you will need to make that point crystal clear to any individual or company you hire to do turn-over cleanings for you.

Here are some things to consider when retaining a cleaning service:

Location—How close are they to your STR? You want someone who is close and easily accessible. Someone who is far away will have high fuel costs.

Experience (especially with STR/vacation rentals)—How much experience do they have? And are they familiar with the different cleaning needs that vacation rentals must have?

Communication/ease of Change—How easy are they to get in contact with? Are they responsive? Can they accommodate last-minute requests?

Cost—The lowest cost for cleaning services is not always the best, nor vice versa. You will also need to look at whether you are going to pay by the job or a certain amount per hour. Both have their pros and cons. If you pay by the job, they may be inclined to rush through, and if you pay by the hour, your cleaners might take their sweet time. This is one reason I suggest doing the cleanings yourself, so that you have a reasonable expectation as to the time an average cleaning will take, and ultimately cost. I know I am extremely efficient and fast. Just by reading other's average times of completion, I know it will take someone else longer to clean my properties and therefore, I will need to adjust my cleaning fees should I ever outsource the work regularly.

Reliability—Can you depend on your cleaners to show up when they need to be there and finish before the next guest checks in?

Reviews/recommendations—Always ask for reviews or recommendations from other clients. I frequently had clients I would ask to provide recommendations for my work, and several gave me standing permission to share their contact info with any potential new clients.

Scalability—As you scale your STR business, the least amount of time you spend on scheduling the better. Will your cleaners be able to keep up with new opportunities? If you're still texting/calling maids for every turn-over it's going to be very time-consuming. You also do not want to have to find, vet, and hire new cleaners every time you list new properties.

Basic requirements of a cleaning crew

As a business owner, I make sure that anyone cleaning for me is clear on what I expect of them when they are cleaning one of my short-term rentals. I let them know they should:

- Make all the beds

- Clean and put away any dishes

- Provide a thorough clean of the toilets, showers, and bathtubs

- Empty all trash and recycling cans

- Sweep, mop, and vacuum

- Wipe down counters and high-touch surfaces such as door handles and light switches

The above services are the minimum a cleaning crew should provide. However, as an STR host, you want your property to go above and beyond. When selecting a cleaning crew, look for companies that offer these additional services, either within their flat rate or as add-on packages:

- Deep cleans: once a month, a cleaning crew does a thorough clean of the entire property that includes those "hard to reach" places.

- Washing linens: Providing a laundry service will ensure there is always a fresh pair of sheets for each bed.

- Help with property damage: If the crew notices damage to the property, they will communicate it to the host, take photos, and potentially create a temporary solution. I suggest your cleaning crew take photos of the space between every guest.

- Report inventory: Hosts often provide the cleaning materials, and can lose track of what is remaining. A cleaning crew can report back to the host when the inventory is low.

Whether you are cleaning your STR, outsourcing, or a hybrid between the two, keep in mind that your reputation as a host can rise or fall depending on the level of cleanliness. It is often the primary source of guest concerns and remains one of the most important parts of running a successful short-term rental. Let's talk now about a few negative situations I have encountered while hosting and how I dealt with them.

When Things go South

———

Sometimes, despite your best efforts, things can and will go horribly wrong at your property and a guest will be unhappy.

When I started out, I was determined that I would avoid this through my years of experience in customer service. Somehow, I would simply never allow there to be problems, and therefore I would never have to worry about a critical review and all would be right with the world.

Hey, a girl can dream!

Reality was a real bummer because things happen. I'll run you through a couple of scenarios that happened in my own properties in a moment, but first let me just preface it by saying that at one point I had issues striking both short-term and long-term rental properties at the same time. It was a stressful week.

How we react to these issues defines our longevity as short-term rental hosts and/or landlords.

Situation #1: Poor internet and a mouse in the house

In early 2020, right after the COVID pandemic hit, we had a couple stay for two nights. They were young and didn't have unlimited data on their phones, so they were quite dependent on our Wi-Fi. Worse, it was winter, the first winter we had been in business as an STR. Each winter, in our house, and in Cottage West, we get an influx of rodents. Now I know how to trap these smart city mice. But at the time I did not. Unfortunately, Cottage West had two mice in it, and they were as bold as can be, so the guest got a snapshot of them and eventually a full refund on their two-night stay.

Lessons learned:

- Invest in all manner of pest control (glue traps *work*)

- Spend the money to get your Wi-Fi at top speed or have a very good reason it isn't offered and state that in your listing and guest handbook (for instance, our Airstream gets poor reception because its metal skin acts as a giant Faraday cage)

Situation #2: Locals book for one night and move their entire apartment in

It was late February 2021, and the temperatures in Kansas City hit a frigid -10 degrees Fahrenheit. It was a miserable, bone-chilling cold, and I received a same-day booking request from a local (their profile on Airbnb said they were from Kansas City) with a note stating that their electricity was out and they needed a place to stay for one night.

We did not have our Ring motion-sensor floodlight and camera in place, just a simple Ring doorbell. The guests covered the doorbell and spent the next few hours moving *their entire two-bedroom apartment into Cottage West*. The following day, I didn't have new guests scheduled to arrive, so I delayed walking over to clean Cottage West. Normally I'm there right after 11 am. checkout to get it done. By noon, an hour after checkout, I received a text from the guests notifying me they were still there. They asked if they could extend one more day. As I was checking my calendar, they suddenly asked if they could stay for ten more days, and every one of my internal alarms whooped, "Danger, Will Robinson, Danger!" I told them I had other guests coming, blocked that evening so they couldn't book, and after waiting for nearly two hours for them to leave, showed up with my husband and "helped them" move out. They had moved in three televisions, dozens of large garbage bags full of belongings, and even decorated with their own little bric-à-brac glass animals!

Three hours later, we had them moved out. Later, my husband found a heroin kit in the drawer of a nightstand. I bought a set of Ring cameras *that day* along with a Ring monitoring membership (unlimited devices for $100 per year in monitoring fees).

<u>Lessons learned:</u>

- A Ring doorbell is not enough.

- Question the circumstances more.

- Show up promptly (or have your cleaners there) at the check-out time to clean whether or not you have a guest coming in.

Situation #3: Blackout causes pipes to freeze, burst, and flood Airstream STR with 1,500+ gallons of water

In January 2022, the neighborhood experienced a quick, five-second power outage. Unfortunately, this turned off the space heater we have set at 59 degrees in our Airstream, the one that keeps the RV toasty warm (far warmer than 59 degrees). As the temperatures dropped, the pipes inside of the propane water heater froze and burst. Combine that with the unfortunate reality of COVID hitting our little household, and it was a full day of water pouring at top speed out of the Airstream before we realized it. Now maybe you don't have an Airstream STR like us. Nevertheless, in cold-weather climates, burst pipes are a common occurrence in winter. The whole debacle cost us around $400—from the large amount of water usage to a new camping water heater (along with expedited shipping), and plumbing parts. We had one guest due to show up on the day we would receive the water heater. I reached out to him, explained the situation and asked him whether he would prefer to keep the reservation or cancel. He kept the reservation, and we installed the water heater before his arrival.

Lessons learned:

- When the power goes out, check the safety systems you have in place.

- Be as proactive as possible with any upcoming guests.

- An extra $25 in shipping to get a part expedited is well worth the money.

Situation #4: Consistent comments and less than five stars about cleanliness until we resurfaced our claw-foot bathtub

Cottage West, our first STR, was put together with blood, sweat, tears, and pretty much every penny we had (and then some). The claw-foot tub was a Craigslist find. Advertised for $50, when I called, the poor guy had apparently had enough of people showing up to buy it and not being able to move it. "If you can move it, it's yours. Free," he told me.

I knew how heavy cast iron tubs were. I grabbed three more strong adults; we piled into our van, and we were there in under an hour. And it was heavy. At least four hundred pounds of heavy! It was also stained. Not horribly, but there were spots in it that, scrub as hard as I could, I simply could not get clean. And this caused me no end of stress in those early days of hosting through Airbnb, where I would see two, three, and four stars for bathroom cleanliness.

As an owner of a housecleaning business, and as the person who handled all the cleanings, I knew things had to be spotless. The stains in that bathtub were hurting my overall rating and threatening to dislodge my Superhost status. We paid for it to be refinished and overall; it was well worth the $350 cost. Yes, I got a 100-plus-year-old bathtub for free and yes, it absolutely was worth the $350 makeover. To this day, it remains the first picture you see in my listing. Many folks tell me it's the reason they booked Cottage West!

Lessons learned:

- To many people, discolored means dirty.

- Keep things sparkling. If they don't sparkle, replace/upgrade them.

Those are just a handful of examples from my own personal experiences. You will encounter issues unique to your situation. I hope the examples above help you deal with them in a professional, yet hospitable manner. More on this in the next chapter—Reviews, Reviews, Reviews!

Reviews, Reviews, Reviews!

———

Why Reviews Are Important

Do you ever shop online? Say, at the mighty Amazon, for example? I'll admit, as busy as my life is, I'm kind of addicted to it. I can find dozens of choices, colors and patterns, as well as competitive prices, all delivered right to my door. What's not to love about that?

Another one thing I love most about it is, when in search for a product, I can clearly see the established, well-loved products which have tons of high reviews. I will choose an item that has 4,000+ positive reviews over something that has, say, 19. The numbers matter. And so do those stars. And while they can buy reviews on places like the great and powerful Amazon, it is far more difficult to do so in places like Airbnb or VRBO. For every review posted, at least one person has stayed at the property, and (hopefully) enjoyed it enough to post a review about it.

It is social proof that you have a place worth considering.

And it's really nice to get reviews like this one...

Tori

Wow! Just wow!! Christine's place is AMAZING!! It's an older neighborhood with charm but when you enter the home you are in a whole new world. Christine literally thought of EVERYTHING!! I felt like maybe Mary Poppins lived there cuz every time I thought of something I needed POOF!! ir was there!! No need or want left unmet! Even when I wasn't sure how to use the vintage items, POOF! there was a framed note with instructions on how to use it. No need to dig through cupboards to search for what I needed cuz they were beautifully labeled with contents. The beds were VERY comfortable and they even left a little note about possible city night noises along with an individually wrapped pair of ear plugs by each bed. See!! They thought of everything!! We were traveling with a dog and they even had a bed in the living room, a kennel in the laundry room and a basket of dishes and such in the kitchen. What a great stay! I highly recommend it!

This kind of review? Where they are gushing over you? That's pure gold, right there. It tells other potential guests several really important things, such as:

- I thought of everything

- I care about my guests' comfort

- I made it easy for my guests to find what they need

- I even thought about their pets

- I channeled my inner Mary Poppins!

If you read that review, would you want to stay at Cottage West? Or would you rather go to a Comfort Inn? That was a rhetorical question, by the way.

That guest just sold my next five guests on Cottage West for me. I don't have to say a thing. Well, except maybe a thank you for such a lovely review.

And while I'm beating my drum, here is another amazing review...

JoAnne

Christine's place was wonderful, as was she. She truly has the gift of hospitality and it was evident in all of the little welcoming touches.

In a world of increasing connectivity and instantaneous reporting, a review can make or break your business. That said, I would caution you to not let yourself get so wrapped up in reviews that you lose your mind over a 4-star (or less) review. Do not allow yourself to fear the occasional negative review because, eventually, no matter how good you are, you will get one, whether it is warranted or not. And when the scammers come along, making up issues where there aren't any (yes, this will happen), don't be so afraid of a critical review that you refund their money. More on this later.

How to Ask for Reviews

Not every guest is going to leave a review for you, and that is perfectly okay. It isn't required of them, just as it isn't required of you. I faithfully leave reviews on nearly all of my guests (more on that later), and I gently ask for reviews while wording that request carefully.

You can see my request for a review in the highlighted section below:

Good morning [guest first name]!

This is an automated message sent the morning of checkout.

Checkout is at 11:00 am. If you end up leaving earlier, please let me know so that we can arrange for the cleaners to come. Thank you for staying at Cottage West—I hope your stay was peaceful and comfortable.

You can set any used bath or kitchen linens in the laundry basket in the hallway. There is no need to strip any used bed linens—we handle that. Please do not re-make any beds used. And if you could please wash any used dishes, that would be fantastic! If you are in a hurry, don't worry about it at all.

There is no need to set the alarm. Just press the center button on the keyless entry to lock it when you leave the house.

We would love for you to join our monthly newsletter. You will see the link to that in the note inside the property regarding saving money for future bookings.

We hope you have had a 5-star stay. Please don't forget to review. We are also very open to private feedback on how we can improve the space for your return visit in the future.

Thanks again, and safe travels!

Notice I haven't directly asked for a 5-star review. I've merely stated that I hoped they had a 5-star stay. This is an important distinction. It says, "I've done whatever I can to make the stay as perfect as possible. I hope you agree." And this has been the perfect mix of verbiage for us. We are encouraging them in the nicest way possible to give us five stars without demanding it, and we are guiding them toward giving us any true feedback via the private feedback section. I've also added the suggestion to keep any constructive feedback in the private feedback section. Why private feedback? Well...

Encouraging Private Feedback Versus Public

Why is asking for private feedback important? Look at these two reviews...

Denise
Mar 29 - May 31, 2022
Cottage West · Central Locale Close & Convenient

Overall rating   ★ ★ ★ ★ ★

Public review   Reply ›

My 18 & 21 yr old kids and I come to KC every 3 months at least. We will never stay elsewhere! this truly felt like "home" immediately! The level of detail in both labeling and what you might need or enjoy is absolutely incredible! Christine has outdone herself! She & Dave were super responsive, welcoming, and easy to work with! the little touches from charging cords to personal notes in the books, from the fun quirky signs to the history of this property, from a crate and a dogbed, there was nothing left to want!

Private note

this old back would love a firmer mattress lol... i've yet to find one anywhere away from home! i'm a huge ice user, just fyi all the ice trays were empty...a freezer tray/bucket might come in handy...i have a spare if you want one in june lol we go, so, so look forward to coming back... you've really thought of everything!!

Here Denise has written an amazing public review. She has also let me know, "Hey, I found your mattresses a bit too soft. And you really need to monitor the ice trays, or have a full ice bucket."

I immediately ordered an ice bucket for the freezer on Amazon and resolved to check the ice trays at each cleaning. It was something I had gotten out of the habit of during the winter since I only use ice when it's summer. That's not true of everyone, though, so it makes sense to take 30 seconds out of a cleaning to check on that.

Let's look at Reid's review now...

Reid
Apr 6 - Apr 6, 2022
Cottage West - Central Locale Close & Convenient

Overall rating ★ ★ ★ ★ ★

Public review   View reply ›
5-stars from us for this stay! Christine's home was wonderfully appointed, in a convenient location not far
from the heart of Kansas City. Loved all the fun touches in the home, and that it retained lots of original
details like the distressed wood floor and clawfoot tub. Off-street, gated parking was appreciated, as well
as having a side yard to take the pups out for potty breaks. Thanks again for opening your home to us,
Christine!

Private note
All was swell with the stay! A couple notes for potential areas to look into: We slept in the bedroom to the
left (the tall bed frame). The mattress/frame seemed to cave a little in the middle, so we'd find ourselves
migrating that direction when sleeping. I heard some sounds in the bedroom in the early AM) that were
reminiscent of a recent experience we had at our cabin by Mount Rainier, where a little mousey visitor was
scratching wood inside the walls. Not sure if that was what we heard at your place, but may be worth
setting some traps in the attic, and doing a walkthrough of the perimeter of the house to scan for potential
ingresses. Again, all in all, a wonderful stay. Thanks again for opening your home to us!

Another lovely, 5-star review for the public to read. But Reid echoed Denise on the mattress concerns and let me know we might have a mouse problem. Yikes!

It actually turned out to not be mice, but a far bigger problem. The brick facade was buckling out and away from the house, allowing a gap between the wood frame and brick wall. Local birds took advantage of this and nested between the wood and brick facade. Not mice, nevertheless, I'm glad for that feedback. We got it fixed before it became a real problem.

Here is what I love about these private notes, and it goes back to my belief that most people are kind and want others to succeed. Treat them right, and they will return the favor. Both Reid and Denise wrote fantastic, kind, and thoughtful 5-star reviews of Cottage West. However, they wanted me to know about things they felt needed improvement. Not just for their return stay, but for others who would come after them.

And while you can't always go out and buy a new mattress based on a couple of reviews, it is worth putting toward the top of your wish list for future improvements. I asked for their feedback, and they gave it. It's now up to me to improve the property in the small or big ways that they have suggested.

Private feedback gives a fair amount of grace to a host. The guest can say, "Hey, you need to improve or fix this." And it isn't a public shaming. Instead, it is constructive criticism. Yes, there really is a place for constructive criticism!

Encourage your guests to help you improve as a host through the use of private feedback and try to be open to what they say. Remember, you don't need to change something just because one person complains. I recently had someone complain about the microfiber towels being uncomfortable. This is the first review I've had that has complained about them, and until I hear more, I won't run out and buy different towels when it might not be an issue for anyone else.

And remember...

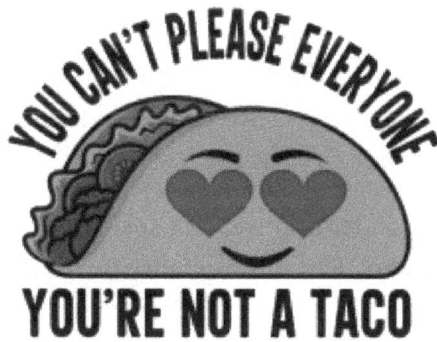

Posting reviews on guests

Reviews are not a one-way street and I encourage you to write a review on every guest you host, whether they respond in kind.

Why posting reviews on guests is important—Reviews are just as important for guests as they are for hosts. They are, again, social proof of who you will be hosting. A stranger is coming into your home. Are they trustworthy? Will they be respectful of your property? Are they a nightmare guest (i.e., demanding, high maintenance, destructive)? Will they smoke in your non-smoking property? Others are depending on you to help them decide on whether to allow someone into a property they have worked hard on and usually invested thousands of dollars (if not far more) into.

<u>What's important (and what isn't)</u> - I've seen some pretty detailed reviews from hosts. Agonizing detail, in fact.

"This guest broke three of our fifteen rules. They ate in the bed. There were crumbs everywhere! Used every towel in the house. Didn't wash all the dishes and the ones he did were not washed correctly and there was sticky residue on all surfaces. He also refused to use the coasters and left wet glass rings everywhere. They did not strip the beds per our checkout rules, the trash was overflowing, and they shaved and left hair ALL OVER the bathroom."

These details, while important to this host, are unnecessary. Everyone has varying levels of cleanliness, and they may be starkly different from your own. As someone who ran a cleaning business for over 15 years, I understand this far better than most. I've seen the insides of people's houses when they didn't remember you were coming to clean, and let me tell you, the complaints above are *nothing* compared to what I've had to muck through regularly!

Digging into the weeds and listing every sin are hallmarks of a host who does not understand hospitality. Part of hospitality is cleaning up after someone else. No one, and I repeat, no one, needs a list of issues a host had with a guest other than a quick synopsis of the problem. Instead, try something like this:

"[Name] caused significant damage (two throw rugs and a comforter) and smoked inside of the property. Regretfully, I cannot recommend [name] to other hosts."

What do you, as a host, want to know about a potential guest? I want to know if there have been problems, damage, or issues of any kind. Past that, I don't really care if they are overly hairy, prefer horses to people, or if orange is their favorite color. Does this guest have a good track record? Awesome, then they can stay. Will they host a "taco party for the maintenance guys" (actual quote from a host review) that includes hamburger ground into the carpet and the leasing company canceling the host's contract? Nope, I'll pass.

That said, here is a recent negative review I posted on a guest:

"Timothy and his family stayed for two nights. During that time, two rugs were destroyed—shredded, really. There were broken glass shards inside of the freezer. The damages exceeded the income received from the two-night stay. I am sorry to report that I cannot recommend this guest to other hosts."

One thing I forgot to mention in the review was that he also ignored my request for damages. That would have been an important thing to add. I still received compensation from Airbnb's AirCover, despite that, it should have been noted, since that is something I would want to know as a host. If I host this guest, and he damages items, will he make good on it? Before my review, Timothy had a single positive 5-star review. Now he has two, with an average of 3.5 stars. Would you host Timothy?

<u>Keep it simple</u>—I have a standard review that I send out. It rarely varies. If I have had little or no difficulties with a guest, my review goes like this:

"[Name of Guest] was a wonderful guest, and we were happy to host [him/her] at [name of unit]. [He/she] is welcome back anytime!"

That's it. Short and sweet. Obviously, I add their names, and all the other details, into the bracketed areas. Over 99% of my guests receive this and a 5-star review from me. I had a guest the other day who heated something in the toaster oven that caused cheese to drip all over the inside. They still received five stars. Yes, I could have knocked them down to three or four stars for cleanliness—but I chose not to. Unless I'm going to detail it in the review, it simply isn't worth it. Also, I'm happy to have them return, cheese mess or not, as I consider that basic cleanup.

How to learn from an inevitable critical review

You will get critical reviews. You will get 4-star, 3-star, even 2-star and 1-star reviews.

It *will* happen.

Deserved or undeserved, it does not matter. A critical review is inevitable because we are human and imperfect, and we host other imperfect humans (who can also sometimes be jerks). Here are a few examples of how human nature (and other unforeseen circumstances) may cause a poor review:

- A mouse gets in through an open door and runs across the room when a guest is there.

- Your previous guest brought in fruit infested with fruit flies that take a week to completely kill off.

- The internet goes down. Heck, the power/water/gas goes down.

- A snowstorm obliterates parking and access to your driveway.

- You get sick or are out of town and have others fill in and they don't do the job you would do.

Things happen.

We are in the service industry, so when there is anything less than a stellar performance (heck, often even if you haven't done a single thing wrong), you can receive a negative review.

And when these happen, we need to take them in, recognize what is our fault and what is not, and take steps to avoid further negative reviews in the future if, and only if, change is warranted. Occasionally, we can challenge a critical review (critical review does not mean 4 stars, folks), and I'll talk about that more in a moment.

I mentioned the Wi-Fi coupled with mouse situation in the previous chapter, When Things go South. A poor review was expected, and while it stung, I knew it was coming. There were two issues—or failures, if you will—that caused the guest (and us) frustration. The internet, which is at the far end of the large yard inside our own house, was having trouble supporting all devices. We were in the middle of the first wave of COVID and not only was I at home, but so was my teen daughter (attending Zoom classes while her school remained 100% virtual), my husband (who provides IT support to around 90 users), myself, AND our guests. The smart TV worked fine, but the guest had terrible Wi-Fi reception on their phone while at Cottage West. And in the middle of dealing with that, the *gue*sts sent a photo of the mouse and stated that they expected to see a refund of sorts for their stay.

I offered to refund them that night's stay and let them find other lodgings. They declined. Because of this, I did not issue them a refund. I did not ask what they would consider reasonable. The one time I had done that, and issued a refund, I had still received a negative review *even after the guest had named their "price" and received it.* Guests who ask for refunds know that hosts, especially Airbnb hosts, fear their ratings will slip and that they will lose business, so the hosts try to pay guests off. And this is the way many guests game the system and end up staying at places for free. They then leave a less-than-stellar review, publicly cataloging all the problems they encountered, and the host ends up earning less *and* having a black mark on their record.

I had also seen quite the pattern by reading other hosts' posts on several STR Facebook pages I frequented. The guest would demand a refund or some amount back, receive it, and still post the scathing review. No, thank you!

Instead, I spent $500 purchasing a high-end Wi-Fi extender I could find, sticky traps, mouse bait, and more to prevent the rodent infestation from continuing. I wanted to *fix* the problems, not throw money after a guest who would still leave a critical review and never return.

I knew I had more than enough positive reviews lined up so that a bad one would hurt, but it wouldn't dislodge my Superhost status on Airbnb or lessen my 4.9-star average to a dangerous level. And sure, there is always the chance I was wrong and that the guest would have given me a stellar review if I had refunded their stay, but keep in mind the following...

The Best Advice You Will Ever Receive

I'm going to share with you the best advice I ever received. Back in 2005, I started a housecleaning business. I read up on it, planned how I would offer value to my clients, and began advertising. As I found my first cleaning clients, and built my business, it devastated me when one of them broke off the contract abruptly, without explanation other than "it's not working out." I spent days agonizing over what I could have possibly done wrong until my husband's co-worker gave me this advice: "Don't worry about the clients you lose; focus on the ones you have."

Like I said in the beginning of this chapter, you will get a negative review. It absolutely will happen. Focus on learning from it, fixing and improving what you can, and then let it go. Focus on giving the guests that you have the best possible experience you can.

Right before I wrote this last bit, I stopped and sent the following message to my current guest at Cottage West: "Hi Kevin! Just checking in to see how your stay is going. Are you comfortable? Is there anything you need? Let us know if you need any recommendations for dining destinations!"

Focus on the guests you have now. Be professional. Be kind and friendly. And let all the negative crap go. Seriously. Perfection is an illusion. Don't let it keep you up at night worrying. Karma has a way of biting those folks on the ass, anyway.

How to Respond Publicly to a Bad Review

Let's talk first for a moment about what NOT to say in response to a critical review...

Don't escalate, insult, or call names - I had a guest send me a message via Airbnb after checking out. It said something to the extent of, "I woke up with a rash and I saw a mouse run across the floor. How do you care to respond to that?"

Now, by the time I received the message, I was already at the property, which reeked of weed and cigarettes, the second I stepped inside. Since our property is non-smoking, and I had seen literally this exact guest message word-for-word splashed across several Airbnb Host Facebook sites with hosts talking about scams that guests will try, I knew I had a dirty player on my hands. Whether she had pulled this crap before or just been told by a friend to try it to get a free stay, I am unsure, but I nipped it in the bud.

I responded with a photograph of a blunt they had neglected to dispose of and responded, "I think you should know smoking inside of Cottage West is strictly prohibited and carries a $100 additional cleaning fee."

Her response?

"Oh, yeah, okay cool. Let's let bygones be bygones."

Uh huh.

I never tried to collect on the $100 additional cleaning fee. Instead, I posted a 1-star review of her, and she never reviewed me, likely because she was kicked off of the platform shortly after that.

I saw a host post a reply to someone's poor review and call the guest a "liar who posts lies and more lies." If you were a potential guest and saw this, what would you think? The host shows no hesitation in calling people names and labeling them. Are we in grade school? After saying the guest is a liar, will that be followed up with the age-old "you have cooties?" At worst, there are some serious things wrong with that STR and you do *not* want to stay there. At best, the host is overly sensitive to criticism and is unwilling to recognize there may be some improvements needed to elevate her STR to guest expectations. Don't do what that host did. Do *not* engage a guest in a verbal battle or call someone a liar. Instead, respond professionally and, if you can, with empathy and compassion.

If possible, ignore it—When I say "if possible," that is with the understanding that, after 500+ reviews, it takes a lot for a negative review to hurt my overall rating. When you look at the listing for Cottage West, you will see raving reviews, so the occasional guest whinging about something that is often out of my control (the neighborhood, for example), does not hold a candle compared to all the positive reviews. However, when you are new, every review is important. We often allow our pride to get wrapped up in it all, and I advise you to fight the urge to respond with anything resembling anger or frustration.

Respond calmly and professionally—Consider writing something like this...

"Thank you [name] for your review. I am sorry we could not resolve the situation to your satisfaction. I understand that you were frustrated by [list issue that upset guest] and I am truly sorry we could not come to a solution that you felt satisfied with."

That's pretty generic. There are ways in which you can address the issues the guest had, while gently and surreptitiously tossing them under the metaphorical bus. This gives other hosts a heads-up on poor actors.

I posted this review on a fellow host, one who stayed all of twenty minutes before messaging me and saying that the neighborhood did not feel safe. A few hours later, she requested most of her reservation back, stating that she "preferred to keep her feedback private." She had not canceled, and I could not re-book the property or try to salvage the situation, so I denied her request.

This is what I posted for her review...

Unfortunately, Danielle stated that she did not feel comfortable and left before I could help in any way. Unfortunately, she did not cancel the reservation, and I was unable to offer her any recompense if another person booked. Three hours after arriving and departing she asked for a significant amount of the reservation back and stated she would "prefer to keep her feedback private." As a fellow host, she should recognize how that sounds, "Give me my money back and I won't leave a bad review." That is against Airbnb standards and conditions. Hundreds of guests have stayed with us in the past three years we have been in operation. And my reviews speak for themselves.

This walks the knife's edge, folks. I would not suggest it. While I knew better, I was also grumpy over the whole "bad neighborhood" thing. I live here, and I get a little defensive when folks comment negatively, even while I understand their concerns. I should have kept it far simpler, and more kind, despite her words and actions.

<u>If you suspect a critical review is coming</u>—Perhaps in your interactions with the guest, you are concerned they will leave a critical review. Here is what I, and many other hosts, suggest: delay posting your review until the review period (usually 14 days) is nearly up. Why? Airbnb lists reviews in order of date of stay, so if you wait and post at the last minute on the 14-day mark, if you have had at least four to six stays in the interim that reviewed positively, and the guest's negative review will not show up on the first page of reviews on your listing. If you have had as many as I do in a two-week period (up to 14 guests since most are here for one night) they won't see it on the second page of reviews either. This is important, since any potential guests who are reading your reviews may not see it at all. Here is the review part of the Hedy Lamarr property listing on Airbnb...

Those were my six most recent stays. That's as far as most guests will go to dig into reviews on a listing. If you delay posting your own review of a guest until that time, and you have a relatively short turnover rate between guests like I do, their negative review has less impact on you since most potential guests will never see it.

As I've mentioned, I live in a neighborhood in transition, one that is lower income, although gentrifying quickly. Occasionally, I will have a person who fears the neighborhood and does not wish to stay. In cases like that, I don't refund unless I receive a booking in their place. I know they may have something negative to say, so I delay reviewing them until the 14th day, or sometimes not at all, and then just respond to their low review publicly and as professionally as possible. I recommend you do the same.

How to handle blackmail—Blackmail. Now there's a nasty word.

When I received a text from a guest stating that they "really wanted to give me a positive review" but felt "some discount for all the problems [they] had experienced" was in order—I ceased communicating with them.

It was blackmail, no bones about it, and said that the guest knew enough about the rental platform we were on (hint: Airbnb) to know that anything less than a 4-star review was incredibly damaging and that they wanted me to give them a free stay for a 5-star review.

Here's the problem with that. Even if you were willing to buy them off, there's no guarantee that if you gave them ALL of their money back, they would leave you a 5-star review. In fact, they could take the discount or refund or whatever you gave them and still leave a 1-star review.

When I get that message, I know to leave the guest a low review at the last possible minute (14 days with Airbnb), check the "no" button on whether I would ever host them again, AND report them to Airbnb. And then I take the hit.

In the end, the string of positive reviews overwhelms the odd dirty dealer.

Your other option is to get them to say it, in writing, that they will give you a 5-star review for a discount. Now, you can't *ask* them for that, they have to volunteer it. But you could write something to the extent of, "So, are you saying that if I issue you a refund, you will write a 5-star review?" Here you are simply parroting their words back to them. If they say "yes," cease to communicate with them. When they leave a negative review, which they usually will, simply challenge the review as being against Airbnb's terms of service (more on that below).

What to do About an Inaccurate Review

The longer you are in business, the more likely it is that you will receive an inaccurate review, or one that you feel is unfair, or even retribution for some perceived failure on your part as the host. These can be maddening, as it is often nothing you have control over. There are ongoing threads on the Facebook STR hosts groups on this subject. "My last guest complained about sand and dust. Our property is in the desert!" Or "A guest complained it smelled too much of pine. Our cabin is in the middle of a pine forest." We live in a city, with all the craziness that can entail—that doesn't stop guests from freaking out over police sirens. These, while maddening, will not be removed. Frankly, anyone reading the review will probably think the guest is an idiot, but still, they can rankle.

Others, however, can be downright harmful. If a guest lies, for example, about the level of cleanliness or availability of amenities, sometimes you can get a review removed. I had a guest who booked our Airstream for one night, got her dates mixed up, ignored every message I sent, and showed up the following day. When I showed her that she didn't show up on the correct day, she wanted a full refund. When I would give that to her, she asked for the cleaning fee back. I didn't have cameras mounted near the Airstream, so I hadn't known if she had stayed or not. Some people are incredibly clean, so I performed the normal turn-over, washed the sheets, the works. I told her this, but refunded her the cleaning, anyway. She was so mad that she had screwed up the dates, and I hadn't given her a refund that she posted a one-star review. I challenged it, pointing out that she had given me a one-star rating for cleanliness, but never stepped foot inside the Airstream. Airbnb sided with me and removed her review.

Understand the TOS—Understand the terms of service and use that to your advantage. Has the guest stated in correspondence that they intend to give you a critical review if you refuse to refund them? That's an automatic violation of most, if not all, online booking platforms' terms of service.

Talk to customer service—Reach out to your hosting platform's customer service department and be prepared to quote the specific section of the terms of service that you believe have been violated. It helps if you can submit evidence of that violation through photos, screenshots, etc. A brief word of advice here—be polite and kind, because these reps get a lot of abuse (I used to be in customer service). As the saying goes, you catch more flies with honey than vinegar.

<u>Rinse and repeat</u>—If the first customer service rep is unresponsive, and you still feel the review was unfair, call/chat/email again. You may very well get a different rep with a different answer.

<u>Let it go</u>—If after one (or more) attempts at having the review removed has failed, let it go. Honestly. It is better to focus on the guests who will arrive today, tomorrow and next week rather than one lone disgruntled one who you will never see again. Focus on upping your game so that those who gush compliments vastly outnumber the complainers.

Social Media Presence

———

You don't have to use social media if you don't feel comfortable with it, but it can be a great promotional tool. It is just another way of getting your STR out there, in front of a unique set of eyes. There isn't one platform I can recommend over another—it really comes down to preference. Pick a platform, one that you are comfortable with. If you like, pick two.

Platforms to consider are:

- Facebook

- Instagram

- Twitter

- TikTok

- Pinterest

Hopefully, you have a basic idea of who your ideal guest is. Whether that is families/couples, business travelers, large groups, or a younger audience, connecting through social media can help lead more guests to your STR. Depending on your target guest, you may wish to focus on certain social media apps where you will have the highest audience. This 2022 report details usage of social media apps by age range...

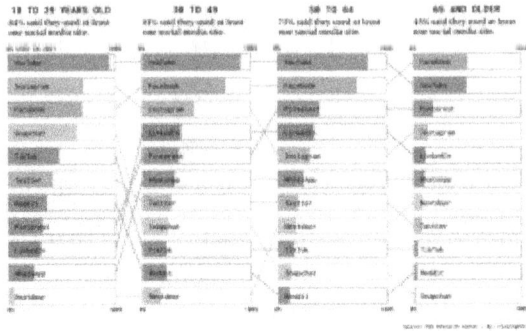

I have a Facebook business page for The Cottages and also an Instagram account. I use them differently.

I have shared my Facebook business page with my Facebook friends and I also encourage guests to join as well. I use it mainly to share reviews and blog posts. This has worked well for local reach, as many of my contacts refer their friends and family to stay at Cottage West and even the Hedy Lamarr Airstream. I blog rarely on the Cottages website. When I do, it is usually food/event/destination-related or a recent addition/update to our offerings, and it makes sense to share it on The Cottages Facebook page.

For my Instagram account, which is called The Cottages Art Spot, I typically focus on art that my guests have created on the blackboard tables I have in each of the STRs. I might also include photos of hand-written notes and reviews that guests have written in the guest book in each location.

The reach is not a huge one, but my posts do occasionally garner comments like this one...

I think you are the best. I worry because so many other AirBnBs are so sub par. When we traveled we tried booking others in Texas & Louisiana & they were far more expensive than hotels with a huge list of chores & conditions & somehow a $100+ cleaning fee. Sorry, but if you want me to do my dishes, laundry, take out trash & vacuum you best not dare to charge me. You are 10000x better than everyone else. You are a shining star in their sky. Keep up the amazing work.

Which serves to point out another huge failing of so many STR hosts: charging *more* than hotels, *including a cleaning fee*, and expecting guests to do a long list of chores. Again, we are in the *hospitality* business, folks. Charge top dollar if you wish, but don't include a list of chores to go with it. Most tried-and-true STR guests will clean up after themselves as a matter of course, but a long list of "to do's" will sour them quickly. I recently had a guest write the following review, which I happily shared on The Cottages Facebook account...

Here's what Maggie wrote

Maggie

We really liked the cottage! I appreciate that Christine was super responsive to messages and that she provided so many things above and beyond what other places do. For example there are ear plugs to address the street/city noise, feminine hygiene products, extra toothbrushes, flossers, disposable razors, blow dryer and more. The home was comfortable and a great place to relax every night. I also love that it is dog friendly and a crate and pet bowls are provided! We didn't bring our dog on this trip but if we get a chance to come back I would stay here again. The yellow porch was a nice place to stretch in the morning sun and I love that yoga mats were available for that as well. It was also refreshing to not be charged an unreasonable cleaning fee, and we didn't have a chore list of things to do at check out other than common courtesy tasks (putting dirty dishes in the sink).

When posting to social media, think about what you want to convey to potential guests. What do you want them most to know? What makes your space one that they absolutely have to stay at? And more than that, what is in the area that would appeal to them?

While I don't particularly have a large reach through social media, as with anything, these things take time and effort. Promoting your space successfully often includes focusing on the region you live in, not just your particular STR. Think about the amenities, then profile them in images and posts. Also, consider adding yourself to local area event notifications. Recently, we had a homes tour close by. A group of six homes were on the tour, and I made sure our guests knew about it. You could create a newsletter to send out as well, highlighting local events and happenings to draw return guests.

Part VII: Money Matters

The Art of the Upsell

You have this amazing space and you are hopefully finding it filled regularly with guests. Your income is where you need it to be to pay for this endeavor and make you a decent amount of cash, but now what?

Why not offer some kind of up-sell? Whether it is a snack basket or a piece of art, or a painting your talented cousin has created, what can you offer besides your short-term rental? Your guests are right there, ready to spend money on food, activities, and more. Take advantage of it!

Perhaps you are a writer, like me, or an artist or creative entrepreneur. Perhaps you live on a farm, or are near a farm. Are you in a touristy hub where you could offer scuba diving to your guests, or special tours of a particular landmark? Are there other small businesses or artisans you could contract with?

The possibilities are endless. I will suggest a few, some of which we do now or plan for in the future.

Upsell #1—Early or Late Checkout

Maybe I'm a pushover, because I offer this for free to guests, but offering an early or late checkout ahead of time could be a benefit to your bottom line. And while, yes, it can be a great freebie to offer guests and I'm not saying you shouldn't, it can also be a lucrative extra benefit, one that can earn you a slight bump in income if you feel it fits for you.

Guests sometimes arrive early from a flight, or a long car ride, and they are more than willing to pay some extra money to get in the place early. It is definitely something to consider. And if you *don't* charge for this, it is still a great bonus for the road-weary traveler if you were to offer it for free.

Upsell #2—The Creative Entrepreneur—Wait, That's ME!

Products for sale on property:

- Signed copies of all of my paperbacks priced at $15 each (same as Amazon, but signed—what a deal!)

- Random books on bookshelves with a "pay what you want" honor system

- Plans for bottles of home-brewed mead for sale by 2025

As of mid-2022, I have written twelve books (this one is my lucky number 13!), with plans for at least two dozen more. I keep a small stock of paperback copies available, signed, and sitting on the shelves in all of our STRs. The picture above is of the first set of shelves I had for my books. Once I added more, I had to switch to two long shelves to hold them all. I keep one copy of each book on hand for sale in Cottage West, along with a QR code pasted to the wall behind the book that gives guests all the links necessary to purchase an e-book version on their favorite bookselling platform.

I also have older formats (different covers/versions) available and scattered throughout Cottage West, our first short-term rental. Those copies, along with a conglomeration of cross-genre books stuffed into multiple bookshelves, are basically on the honor system and I provide a tip jar and encourage people to take a book and either leave one or leave a tip "for the book fairy."

Not a single person has left with a signed/sealed book and not paid. However, I recommend you photograph an area where you have items for sale in order to provide some kind of documentation in order to recoup costs through an online booking platform if a guest helps themselves and refuses to pay. In 2021, I earned around $200 in sales for the entire year. In 2022 it was around $450. It isn't a huge amount of money, but it is a nice little bonus. My book sales will grow the more books I write. And I have plans for a lot more books!

Soon, we will have a meadery in place and bottles of mead (honey wine infused with fruits) for sale. Our property, while in the city's heart, spreads over one acre and we grow elderberry, as well as cherry, apple, and pear trees we can use when creating meads. My husband is hard at work on Back Alley Meads and that will be a lovely item for guests to purchase from The Cottages soon. We could even expand this to include an Airbnb Experience of "Brew for the Day" to our guests and help them learn how easy home-brewing can be.

Are you a writer, artist, indie filmmaker, or sculptor? Perhaps you make handmade quilts (or know someone who does). Art? Collages?

I recently bought some sliced wood pieces in just the right size for a coaster and drew this...

I'm considering creating a pack of four, tying them with twine and selling them for $10. I can set them on a shelf and have yet another easy and potentially profitable upsell for guests.

Upsell #3—The Host in the Know

Do you know all the cool places to hang out and have extra time on your hands? This might be the perfect gig for you. Put together a list of great places to show your guests for a reasonable fee and consider making brochures. Most don't want a big sell, but it doesn't hurt to mention that you offer a service that guests might want to use. Even better, see if you can negotiate some better pricing for them in exchange for the extra business you are steering towards your favorite scuba-diving shop or winery.

In August 2021, my husband and I flew to Austin, Texas to enjoy a weekend away, and we booked our stay in an Airstream Airbnb. A few days after booking, Airbnb sent us a link to its Experiences page, and I spent some time reading up on cool activities that other Airbnb hosts are creating—like a boozy float trip down the river with transportation and beer provided!

Our neighborhood has many historic homes. A walking tour of the area, or even a tour on electric scooters, could be quite fun for guests visiting our area.

Curated experiences, based on your intimate knowledge of your area, can be fantastic and just what visitors are looking for. What do you know about the surrounding area? What do you find fun to do? How can you use your own unique talents and knowledge to create an experience your guests won't soon forget?

Upsell #4—The Movie Package or S'Mores for the Glampers

We offer Netflix, Hulu, and Amazon Prime to our guests. There are plenty more online stream services to choose from that we might try out in the future... HBO Max, Showtime, Sundance, just to name a few.

Why not package up some great snacks (microwaveable popcorn, a handful of different boxed candies), wrap them in cellophane, and sell them for $10 or $15 there in the unit?

Or if your property is a wilderness or camping/glamping type property and you can keep the chocolate from melting, consider making s'mores packages for your guests.

Upsell #5—Equipment Rentals

Bicycles, surf boards, scooters, skis—the sky is the limit here. Even cars can now be rented out on Turo (or EasyCar in the UK)

Upsell #6—Kids' Packs

After a long day of traveling, parents are exhausted and kids are stir-crazy. Why not provide a "Kid-Tainment" basket with some cute, inexpensive activities? Our local Dollar Tree, where everything is one dollar, comes to mind. Put together five to six items, wrap it in clear cellophane, and charge $10-$15 for the package. The kids will love it and their parents will be thankful that the little tykes are busy playing.

Upsell #7—For the Home Chef

Are you a wizard in the kitchen? Do you love to bake? Bonus points if you have specific aptitude in a particular cuisine. Thai, Italian, Indian, Middle

Eastern—the sky is the limit! During the winter, I love to make soup. Add a note to the dining table detailing what you offer and the price. If you are close by, and willing to either whip something up or perhaps you have it on hand (or frozen and ready to defrost), you could easily incorporate upselling meals to your hungry guests!

Upsell #8—Local Tastes

Kansas City is well-known for its local barbecue and for its up-and-coming breweries and distilleries. What about your area? In the months to come, I'm planning on putting together a couple of different packages for travelers to purchase. A BBQ pack, with more flavors of sauce than guests could sample in a two or three-day stay, could really be a winner!

Upsell #9—Mid-Stay Cleaning

I specialize in shorter stays, as I have mentioned several times. You may prefer/specialize in longer ones. And what would be nicer than offering something similar to what hotels offer with housekeeping? Consider offering a mid-stay cleaning for a reasonable rate. It might not be the full cleaning rate you would charge for a stay, perhaps shave off a little, but it is a lovely option to offer your guests who might be there for two or three weeks at a time. It also can help mitigate the length of a cleaning at the end of a long stay.

Pro Tips

- Keep your inventory simple and easy to track. For example, I only set out one of each of my books for sale and I have a little QR code directly behind each book so that I can quickly tell if a book is missing.

- Clearly label the item as being for sale and consider putting it up out of reach of small hands.

A Short Note on the Honor System

Forbes has a great article on how the honor system works and more. Check it out at: https://bit.ly/3qp0ulb.

In summary, adding at least one or two upsells to your property can really make a difference to your bottom line and add something that your guests will really appreciate.

Next, we will talk about some of the top business tax write-offs.

Top Business Write-Offs for STRs

W hen you are operating an STR, you are operating a business and you should treat it as such. One of the best ways to make sure you are keeping as much of your income as possible—is through business write-offs on your taxes. These reduce your tax burden and allow you to continue to re-invest in your properties. Of those write-offs, there are the standard ones, and then there are more rental-specific ones to keep in mind. I'm going to give you a basic rundown of tax write-offs for your STR business, but please keep in mind that I'm not a tax consultant or an accountant (nor do I play one on TV). Here are some standard business write-offs:

Travel Expenses—If you drive to your rental property, you can deduct the percentage of fuel, service, insurance, and car payment expenses you have dedicated to your business. Say you drive 20,000 miles in a year, and 5,000 of that is STR-specific (visiting the STR, running errands to buy supplies, etc.), your usage is around 25% business and 75% personal. This adds up! Also, travel to conferences specifically related to your STR business can be counted as well. That includes airfare and accommodations.

Meals and entertainment—If you provide co-host services and are wooing a property owner you want to do business with, keep your receipts for this exemption. The same if you end up purchasing a meal for an employee, sub-contractor, or a guest.

Office expenses—Need a new printer, scanner, computer for your business? Even if you are spending money on smaller items, such as printer paper, staples, et cetera, we can write them off under office expenses.

Co-hosting Expenses—Do you split your profits with a co-host? If so, you definitely need to keep track of it for your end-of-year taxes. Just as with a cleaning service, this is a write-off for you and a taxable item for your co-host. If you don't track it, you could be on the hook for 100% of the earnings, whether or not they have all gone to you.

Depreciation expense—Here is a cool little tidbit I learned on depreciation. Residential properties depreciate over 27.5 years, while non-residential properties depreciate over 39 years. If your short-term rental only averages 30 days or fewer as an average rent period, it would classify as transient. It is therefore classified as a commercial property and depreciates over 39 years.

The above are standard business deductions you can claim on your taxes. That isn't where it ends, however! STRs have other expenses that can be written off as expenses come tax season. Let's take a look...

Cleaning Services—Anyone you hire to clean your property, whether it is an individual or business, is a tax write-off. I only use this once or twice per year for now, but in the future, I hope that when my four STRs are in full swing, I will be in the market for more help. That would be a lot of cleaning to do all on my own, seven days a week!

Insurance premiums—Whether you carry landlord insurance or short-term rental insurance, both types are considered a business write-off.

Lodging taxes—Does your municipality charge lodging taxes? If so, you have another built-in write-off.

Security systems—Installation of burglar alarms, the costs of monitoring them, and even security cameras and monitoring fees are considered tax write-offs.

Renovation costs—Your costs for renovating a property to get it ready to be a short-term rental is also a write-off. If you decide to add a room, even an amenity such as a hot tub, these are considered a write off.

Furniture and supplies—The list is long. Furniture, appliances, and the supplies necessary to stock and run the STR, right down to the toilet paper, are all write offs.

Various other rental expenses—Mortgage interest, property taxes, utilities and more fall under this broad category and can be used as tax write-offs.

Tax write-offs reduce your tax burden and are a great way to mitigate the cost of doing business. This chapter has covered the bare basics and I highly recommend Nolo's *Every Airbnb Host's Tax Guide* for an accurate and up-to-date list of what you can, and what you cannot, use for a tax write-off. Next up, financial tracking...

Keeping Track of Your Financials

———

O kay, this is where I put on my business and accounting hat. In previous chapters, I have talked about a lot of different things—the feelings you want to invoke in your guests, the level of service I advise you provide, even best practices for communication.

While I would prefer a more even spread on platforms, Airbnb currently comprises over 93.5% of my gross short-term rental income. The other 6.5% of my income is spread over multiple platforms. VRBO/Home Away accounts for 2.95%, Trip Advisor 1.04%, and direct bookings from repeat guests hover at around 3.56%. Your area might have a heavy VRBO (or any of the other platforms) presence with guests.

No matter the source, knowing exactly how much is coming in (and especially how much is going *out*) is very important. Without an average daily rental fee, or knowing exactly how much you are earning in occupancy fees versus cleaning fees, or more—you can't make fact-based decisions for your business.

I have taken the spreadsheets I use daily and tried to pretty them up a little for you. That said, they still don't have all the bells and whistles, but they are invaluable for:

- Predicting the potential income for your STR

- Tracking income by platform (Airbnb, VRBO, direct bookings, and more)

- Tracking your expenses and income by year

- Finding out your average daily rental per property

- Creating a monthly budget for your business

- Comparing annual income and expense from year to year

- Planning for future expansion

The **Complete STR Financial Tracking** file is an .ODS file in LibreOffice, an open source and free format that is compatible with Microsoft Excel. It includes the following spreadsheets:

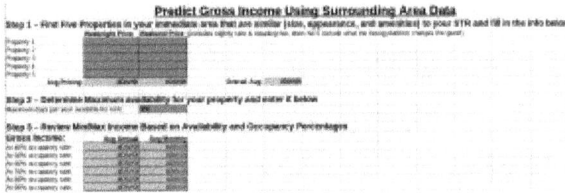

Predicting Income—(you can input data from the surrounding area to determine your gross earning potential)

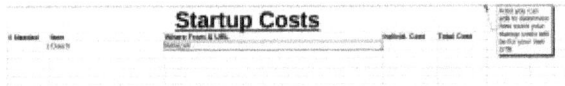

Startup Costs—Where you can put together your own individual startup costs (whether an approximation or actual expense) and know how much you need to roll out your first (or second or third) STR.

Income by Platform—(track earning via the different platforms and know what percentage of your income comes from what source)

Expense and Income—[Year]—(track your income and expenses on a monthly basis over the year)

Average Daily Rental—(track your STR's average daily gross income for lodging and cleaning fees—this will allow you to predict future income for your property)

Your Monthly Budget—(create a budget based on income from the Average Daily Rental sheet)

Profit and Loss by Year—(a year-to-year comparison of your income and expenses)

The **Complete STR Financial Tracking** file is free for anyone who has purchased my book. Simply go to my author website: https://www.christineshuck.com/str-success-resources

One way that I use the **Expense and Income (Year)** spreadsheet is to track on a monthly basis how much I can add to our renovations account. I have set mine to calculate any additional income above our monthly "paycheck" of $3,000. Whether it is $50 or $1,800—I then send that amount out of my business checking and straight into our Renovations Savings account, where it is drawn on as needed for our next two STR renovations, Cottage East and Proud Mary.

Combined with using Quicken Home, Business and Rental Property, I can easily track all incoming and outgoing transactions, prepare for tax time, budget for renovations on new properties, and keep a finger on the pulse of my business.

Taxes and Tax Reporting

A gain, as with the Top Business Write Offs chapter, I am not an accountant or tax expert. Therefore, I highly recommend Nolo's book *Every Airbnb Host's Tax Guide* for an accurate and up-to-date advice on which tax schedule to file. Below is an overview, but it is not intended as tax advice.

Should I File a Schedule C or E?

The short answer is that Schedule C is the form taxpayers have to fill out for active income businesses, while a Schedule E is what investors usually fill out. By looking at the definition alone, you might be confused as to what your short-term rental would be classified as, and this depends on what your involvement in the business is.

Have you hired a co-host to handle all the details for you? Do they handle scheduling maintenance, buying supplies, and supervising a cleaner? Then you likely would want to file a Schedule E, as this is more of a passive/ investment income source.

However, if you are as involved as I am in the day to day running of your short-term rental, then the answer would be to file a Schedule C.

Pros and cons of filing a Schedule E—The biggest advantage of filing your tax returns under Schedule E (the passive income report that applies to rentals) is that you won't be required to pay self-employment taxes on the income reported.

Considering that self-employment is currently taxed at a hefty 15.3% of your income, you can see why many investors choose to file their reports as 100% passive.

But here's the biggest disadvantage of filing the Schedule E form: you'll be limited with writing off tax losses, meaning that the considerable benefits of depreciation will be out of your reach.

You can only write off losses up to your passive income, while the rest will be suspended and continue pooling with no passive loss tax benefits to take advantage of.

Pros and cons of filing a Schedule C—The key advantage of filing under Schedule C is that you'll get to write off losses of up to $25,000 against your active income immediately, dramatically lowering your tax burden and generating more profit.

The catch is that you'll be subject to self-employment tax, which could eat into your profit if you're not calculating all your moves right.

You may qualify as a real estate professional—As a general rule of thumb, all rental income classifies as passive and is required to be filed under Schedule E, leaving traditional landlords with no way of writing off their tax losses in the short term.

The only exception to this is when the landlord qualifies as a real estate professional, meaning that most of their time is spent actively working in the real estate industry, clocking in at least 750 hours per year.

So, where do vacation rental investors fall in all of this?

According to regulations, vacation rental owners who rent their property out for seven days or fewer on average do not fall under standard rental regulations, meaning that they'll be able to file their income as non-passive instead, without worrying about qualifying for professional status.

In the eyes of the law, in fact, investors who fall under the seven-day exception are not running a rental business at all!

This means that investors looking to maximize their rental income can keep their full-time jobs, expand their portfolio, and not clock in any minimum hours while benefiting from depreciation tax write-offs—as long as they are materially participating in the business, of course.

If you are actively managing and marketing your short-term property and qualify for the seven-day exception, you'll be able to use your yearly tax losses to offset your business income and any other income, even if you work a day job.

Finally, should you reach for Schedule E or Schedule C when the end of the tax year comes around?

While you'll be able to claim the biggest benefit of the Schedule C form as a vacation rental owner with seven days or less occupancy, experts recommend using the Schedule E form unless you are providing substantial services to your guests.

Most short-term rentals won't qualify as hospitality businesses, but they can qualify as real estate professionals or non-rental business owners and still get all the depreciation benefits!

What Taxes Booking Platforms Collect on Your Behalf

Per Airbnb, they "automatically collect and pay occupancy taxes on behalf of hosts whenever a guest pays for a booking in specific jurisdictions." You can look your area up by going here:

https://www.airbnb.com/help/article/2509/in-what-areas-is-occupancy-tax-collection-and-remittance-by-airbnb-available. Airbnb says, "Hosts may need to manually collect occupancy taxes[1] in other jurisdictions and in certain listed jurisdictions where Airbnb does not collect all applicable occupancy taxes."

"When we automate this process, it doesn't change which taxes are due or the total payout you receive as a host. You'll continue to receive your payout minus the standard **Airbnb service fees**[2]. Automatic collection and payment simply make tax collection easier for everyone."

1. https://www.airbnb.com/help/article/2496

2. **https://www.airbnb.com/help/article/1857**

Here is an example of what taxes are collected by Airbnb in Missouri, my home state:

Occupancy tax collection and remittance by Airbnb in Missouri

State of Missouri

Guests who book Airbnb listings that are located in the State of Missouri will pay the following tax as part of their reservation:

- Missouri State Sales Tax: 4.225% of the listing price including any cleaning fees, for reservations 29 nights and shorter. For detailed information, please visit the **Missouri Department of Revenue** website.
- City Sales Tax: 0.25%-1.375% of the listing price including any cleaning fees, for reservations 29 nights and shorter. For detailed information, please visit the **Missouri Department of Revenue** website.
- County Sales Tax: 0.25%-6% of the listing price including any cleaning fees, for reservations 29 nights and shorter. For detailed information, please visit the **Missouri Department of Revenue** website.
- Additional County Sales Tax: 0.125%-0.5% of the listing price including any cleaning fees, for reservations 29 nights and shorter. For detailed information, please visit the **Missouri Department of Revenue** website.
- Tourism Tax to Maintain Quality of Water: 0.25% of the listing price including any cleaning fees, for reservations 29 nights and shorter. For detailed information, please visit the **Missouri Department of Revenue** website.
- Promotional Tourism Tax: 0.5%-5% of the listing price including any cleaning fees, for reservations 29 nights and shorter. For detailed information, please visit the **Missouri Department of Revenue** website.
- Local Sales Tax: 1% of the listing price including any cleaning fees, for reservations 29 nights and shorter. For detailed information, please visit the **Missouri Department of Revenue** website.

I recommend searching for this information on each booking platform you end up using for your STR, as the taxes collected could vary by platform.

Taxes That Are Your Responsibility

Any applicable taxes that are not collected by Airbnb and the other online booking platforms will be your responsibility. This includes income tax if you were to file a Schedule C. Obviously, if you are not in the United States, then I strongly advise you to study your country's tax laws or hire an accountant or tax professional to advise you.

Part VIII: A Multitude of Tips

Buying Tips

———

Amazon: You may have noticed that I buy most items on Amazon. This is because of their returns and customer satisfaction guarantee.

Facebook Marketplace: I've found GREAT deals by first finding the price on Amazon, and then checking the Facebook Marketplace. Mattress protectors comes to mind. I purchased three mattress protectors for only $60 versus the $120 or more it would have cost on Amazon. I also found great used furniture on Facebook Marketplace.

Habitat for Humanity ReStore: If you have ever shopped at a thrift store and enjoyed it, then you will probably love visiting a ReStore. The donations come in from everywhere, from individuals, to builders, to hotels renovating their rooms. I especially love the last category, as I can often find matching chairs, nightstands, and wall décor with little or no damage for low, low prices—especially when they get a large delivery. I've bought durable metal dining chairs (from Five Guys locations shutting down) for $5 each and then painted them to match my other décor. I've also purchased comfortable armchairs for my home and my rentals for less than $40 each. The drawbacks are that these deals are catch as catch can. If you have a Habitat for Humanity ReStore in your area, check and see if they have a Facebook page. Ours do and there are at least four to five locations within a 20-minute drive of our home. I get their notifications every day via Facebook. I've also purchased bed frames, appliances, ceiling fans, and, of course, building materials there. Uber-cheap prices and all of their revenues go back to charity!

IKEA: Easy, clean lines and reasonably low prices. If you are on a tight budget, but want something new as opposed to used, IKEA can provide a decent low-to-mid-level look for a reasonable price. Drawback—you will usually need to assemble this furniture yourself, and it can be a real pain in the patoot! That said, we have used plenty of IKEA pieces, as well as purchased sink faucets and curtain hardware from them. If you have one in your area, be sure to check them out!

Zulily: This online company is my go-to destination for quilts and sheet sets. I find them easier to sort through than Amazon, while still having an enormous selection. My favorite finds are their reversible quilt sets. They are thin quilts, definitely not made for huddling under in the deep cold of winter nights, but that actually makes them perfect for my needs. I buy the flannel sheet sets on Zulily as well as the regular cotton blend, and in the winter, the flannel sheets combined with one of the thicker bed blankets keep our guests warm and cozy. I end up using the thin quilts year-round and have two sets for each bed with at least two more backups should I need to hem a seam or treat a stain. Drawbacks include they do charge for shipping, and sometimes the orders can take a while to arrive (at least a week, sometimes two or three).

Beware, Scammers Ahead!

———

Ah, joy of joys, scammers. Wherever money changes hands, you can expect someone is out there, trying to get their hands on it. This manifests in two ways:

When booking—Once you have been doing this for a while, you can see these folks coming a mile away and they are easy to avoid. It's the first couple of times that can be rather unsettling, but they are invariably the same, down to the wording. They usually:

- Request off-platform communications

- Tell you their company is sending a certified check

- Ask for the property address

Request off-platform communications—One of the main reasons a scammer wishes to communicate off-platform is in order to get your personal details, which includes your phone number. However, a potential guest might not think of this and innocently ask since they are more comfortable texting instead of using the listing platform's app. If you are on Airbnb, or one of the other major platforms and you consent to communicate off-platform, you are violating the booking platform's terms of service—and that can get you banned. This does not mean you can't give a guest your phone number, email, etc.—just not prior to them booking or their stay. Communicate this to a potential guest and insist that all communications stay on the platform.

After booking, on the day of their reservation, is the time to release info such as your phone number. There are absolutely times when it makes more sense to call someone rather than text/email. In fact, I've had incidences where a guest had trouble accessing our unit in the dead of night and just left instead of calling us. In our case, the Cottage West Ring doorbell is actually connected to our home and sounds on our Alexa devices. It is enough of a noise to wake us up so we can help, and I advise guests in the Pre-Arrival message to press the Ring doorbell if they need help.

If a guest gives you any kind of problem (such as threatening to leave a critical review unless you give them a refund) off-platform, simply screenshot the conversation and submit it to the platform should you need to contest a review.

<u>Tell you their company is sending a certified check</u>—I have seen dozens of newbie hosts pop up on one of the Facebook host groups and ask if this is a thing. And I have to wonder how many others don't ask and get suckered into this. I don't see this much on Airbnb, but I see it *all the time* on VRBO. It usually starts with an initial inquiry of dates and a brief message like "Hi" or "Is the property available for the dates listed?" Another red flag is the time (sometimes days) that elapses between the initial inquiry and your response and their *second* message, which is always something like this:

"My wife and I would like to book our stay with you and my company will pay for this vacation via a certified check..."

They usually finish this with a request for information. Your name, address, even banking information. Please note: There is *never* a scenario in the STR world where a certified check will pay for anything. So mark it as spam, report them, flag them, whatever. The sooner we ban them, the better. Unfortunately, there will be a dozen more of them waiting in the wings.

And while this has never happened to me, I've read twice about guests contacting hosts, stating there was dirt and more under furniture and suggesting the cleaner they know come and clean, at the host's expense, of course. I literally cannot imagine being taken in by this, but the two hosts who posted separately about this happening, allowed the guest to bring their own cleaner in (although whether a cleaner actually did any cleaning, I truly question) and bill the host for the additional cleaning through the Airbnb platform. That falls under the "I think you have been suckered" category, but hey, apparently it is a scam that works.

<u>What is the property address?</u> - The last one, where they are asking for the address of the property, is not always a red flag, but it can be. Folks occasionally want to know where they are staying, and in most cases, they are fine with waiting until the day of the stay to receive the address and other access details. If you don't wish to give them the exact address, you may wish to list cross streets instead. I usually respond with, *"For security reasons, we do not release the exact address until the day of the reservation. However, our closest cross streets are Benton and Indiana."* In this day and age of Google Maps, it isn't too hard for someone to find the property given cross streets, especially if you have an image of the property exterior, so take my advice with a grain of salt.

Those asking seconds after booking usually get a "you will receive the address on the day of your reservation" response and if they persist and sound as if they are on the up and up, I will release that specific street address early.

There have been instances of guests (usually locals) planning a party. Usually, this is announced via social networks and is an excellent reason to only release the address on the day of the reservation. That way, you can avoid too much advance notice being given.

During/post stay—My favorite, if it can be called that, is the "I woke up with a rash" message. I've only had one group try this. Or the "I saw a mouse" claim. They also threw that in for good measure. I've mentioned this already in earlier chapters. Frankly, if a guest doesn't send an image of an actual mouse, I'm not admitting anything! A claim of a rash, or rodent, when not accompanied by a picture of the little beast, is likely a play for a refund. *Why pay*, a malingering guest might reason, *when I can stay for free*?

I'm not saying that every person who claims to have a problem is lying. Far from it. I think you must take each claim seriously, but also evaluate it for accuracy. With the "I woke up with a rash and saw a mouse" folks, the second I provided evidence of smoking inside of the property, she immediately dropped the claim.

In closing, I have to say this: Most guests are good people who just want a nice place to stay. Most are not scammers out to make a buck, screw you over, or throw a raging party. So... trust, but verify, as the saying goes.

Perform Regular Scheduled Maintenance

———

Regular maintenance of your STR property is one of the oft-neglected areas of rental properties, and it is very important to maintain the value and integrity of your short-term rental. Things wear out, break down, and become rundown without proper maintenance. We often point landlords out as being terrible at maintenance, and for good reason. Isn't it time we changed that dynamic?

After all, nothing in the world of hospitality is "set it and forget it." Not if you want to continue to get great 5-star reviews. And whether you own your own STR, or rent it, maintaining the property, inside and out, is essential to your continued success.

Things wear out. Marks and scuffs appear. Paint gets chipped. Dishes get chipped or scratched. Styles change.

By scheduling regular assessments, where you look at everything with a critical eye, or have someone else you trust to give you a fair, detailed review of all aspects of your STR, you can fix things that need fixing before they get big.

Some things you can never control—your neighbors, the neighborhood at large, the sounds of a city—but what you can control, you should. Remember, we are creating a sanctuary where someone can lay their heads, feel relatively safe, and sleep, bathe, eat.

Are your linens wearing out?

Is the furniture scratched?

Are you missing a spot of paint in an obvious spot?

These are the things that build up over time and add to a general feeling of decline, shabbiness, and open the door for negative comments. Worse, even if you are visiting your STR regularly, they may escape your notice just because of the familiarity of seeing the same thing over and over.

Here are some items to look at on a regularly scheduled basis. It will help keep your property looking fresh and well cared for month after month, year after year. And it will ensure you see reviews like this one...

Here's what Kristin wrote

Kristin

Driving cross country we were looking for a place to rest our heads with the kids and the dog; but, we had no idea the treat that would be cottage west! Dave and Christine are AMAZING!!! They cottage is comfortable, affordable, conveniently located, and has an added bonus of a great yard with off street private parking. It has a "staying at your favorite aunts house" vibe! The Hosts have thought of absolutely everything. There are extras and small reminders throughout that just make you feel at home and so over the top taken care of! They truly love what they do and their guests! Adding this amazing find to our list of places to return to! Such a wonderful experience here at cottage west!

At Each Turnover

A simple assessment. Is everything as it should be? Are there any obvious issues—broken furniture, missing dishes, glassware, or cookware? Pests (ants, rodents, etc.), mold, water damage, broken/cracked windows, electrical, plumbing and heating/cooling issues should all be acted on as soon as humanly possible. These are issues that a guest will notice and comment on negatively when submitting their review.

Monthly to Quarterly

Lights—Check all lights for burned-out bulbs/functionality.

<u>Appliances</u>—Check briefly for functionality. Turn on the stove, toaster, microwave, etc. and just ensure everything works as expected and that the internal lights are functioning.

<u>HVAC</u>—Change furnace filters every eight weeks. Add this as a repeating reminder on your Google calendar so you never forget!

BiAnnual and Annual

<u>Cabinets and doorknobs</u>—Inspecting and tightening the screws on doorknobs and cabinet handles on a semi-annual basis keeps everything in good working order and avoids any rundown appearance.

<u>Count silverware and dishware</u>—Do a quick count of your silverware and dishware. Folks walk away with silverware and dishes can get broken. Bring them up to the expected levels (i.e., service for six or more if you have a six-guest maximum).

<u>Repair/replace</u>—Invest in some furniture stain pens and apply them to any scuffed furniture. Repair or replace any linens that are coming unraveled.

<u>Exterior of property</u>—Check the exterior of your property at least once, preferably twice per year. Are the gutters and downspouts clear of debris? Is there any missing paint, degrading wood that needs maintenance, and is the roof intact? Do you have any overgrown trees that need trimming? Assess your outside furniture, deck, and other outside amenities for any needed repairs or upkeep.

<u>Check safety equipment</u>—Check that the smoke and carbon monoxide detectors are in order by testing them every six months. Annually, replace the batteries with new ones. Double-check your fire extinguisher as well.

<u>Painting</u>—Whatever color scheme you have gone with, scheduling painting touch-ups is essential to maintaining your STR. Guests can be hard on paint. The door frames, cabinets, and anywhere on walls around movable furniture are especially hard hit. You may wish to schedule painting for the fall. The weather is accommodating outside in case you have any exterior painting to do, without the full heat of summer or chill of winter. I'm typically so busy in

the spring with gardening that I simply have no time for painting then! Keep your paint colors well labeled. A spot of paint on the top and side of the can, as well as a label or note written in Sharpie, what room or surface it belongs to will help keep you from making any mistakes. Most times, you can use the time allotted during a turn-over between guests to spot-paint areas as long as you have at least two hours before the next guest is to arrive. Purchasing a low-odor paint is also recommended. Here in the Kansas City area, there are two main home improvement stores—Lowe's and Home Depot. I've found Home Depot's Behr brand paint to be far less noxious than Lowe's, so I don't even need to air the property out when painting. I highly recommend it.

Electrical and Plumbing—An annual inspection of plumbing and electrical is an important aspect of all home maintenance. There are often local companies who will contract with you for an annual or monthly fee to provide these services. This can be essential for preventing issues and also providing ample proof of maintenance to your insurance should some issues or damage occur.

HVAC—Heating, ventilation, and air-conditioning should be checked twice per year. Usually, the spring and fall are perfect times as you move from heating in the winter to cooling in the summer. And again, having a local company provide regularly contracted maintenance of your HVAC system can be essential for preventing issues or showing you have properly maintained it should issues arise.

In summary, performing regular maintenance and status checks will ensure your STR property stays in tiptop shape and continues to provide you with a steady income. Buildings, furniture, linens—they are not static, "put in place and forget about it" kind of things. They are finite and require our attention and consideration. Take care of the details and the property will continue to make you money for years and decades!

The Art of Home Décor

A mid finding the perfect price on comfortable beds and mattresses, lots of us forget the walls of the rooms our guests will occupy. This can be a great opportunity to create a theme in your Airbnb. I summarized different themes in Part II, and you can return to that for some clear definitions of themes. However, I wanted to add a few more tips to the mix. Here goes...

Destination décor—Perhaps you wish to imbue a feel of France, complete with the Eiffel Tower and the Arc de Triomphe, or the iconic cityscape of New York. I created "state" rooms for our short-lived STR south of Kansas City. Each bedroom was a different state—Kansas, Missouri, and California—embracing our locality (we are right on the border of the two states) and our roots (my husband and I met in high school in California).

We already had some lovely prints of the iconic Country Club Plaza in Kansas City in the Missouri room, a couple of framed sketches of Ghirardelli Square and a trolley car from San Francisco, and even a large, framed sunflower for the Kansas room.

Inexpensive options—Wall art can get expensive, so I suggest turning to Etsy.com and looking for downloadable digital art that you can print in various sizes (we use the UPS Store) and then place in an inexpensive frame. You can specify price requirements (I keep them under $7 each) and occasionally hit a sale where you will get up to 25% off of the prints. Once the purchase is complete, you will receive a link to download your purchase. Save it on your computer and then assemble your print order and send it to your local printer. I can find decent frames at Wal-Mart or in bulk packs from the great and mighty Amazon. If I want something other than black or white frames, I will usually disassemble them first and then spray-paint them in a brushed gold or color that works with the room they are going into.

Thrift or up-cycle—If you have a thrift store in your area, check for décor there. Remember, you can always upscale or up-cycle something with a fresh coat of paint. I'm visualizing vases with a coat of metallic spray paint here.

Local artists—If you are artistic in the slightest, here is your chance to shine! It can make attractive to potential guests to mention that your STR is decorated with original art created by the owner. Remember, many people aren't just looking for a place to stay, they want something cool and unique. Have a friend who is an artist? Ask them if they would like to place art for sale in your STR. Review *Part VII: The Art of the Upsell* for ideas on this, but I've seen this used in a multitude of ways in other STR properties, up to and including covering every inch of free wall space with hand-crafted sculptures, paintings, and more.

Incorporate plants—Adding a bit of green into your STR can benefit in multiple ways. They add dimension and depth to a room and a personal touch. And many plants help clean the air. And there are plenty of low-care options for you to consider. I suggest adding any of the following to your STR:

- Succulents—They need infrequent watering and can often handle lower light levels

- ZZ Plant—Can go for months between waterings, it prefers bright, indirect light

- Split leaf philodendron—Water every ten days and it prefers indirect light

- Snake plant—Can also go weeks without water and also prefers indirect light

The spot of green is just what guests need to feel right at home in your STR. For longer stays, I advise leaving notes near the plants advising on their care (this will help avoid over or under-watering).

Listen to Your Guests

G uests are usually your *best* resources for improving your property. Their comments, suggestions and questions can be things that take your place up a notch in the eyes of others. It is one reason I encourage our guests to leave us suggestions in the private feedback. That feedback has led to vast improvements along the way. Here are a few examples...

Promote the side benefits—We have a rather large yard, especially for the city. We have three houses sitting on seven lots, all in a contiguous 250' line along one side of the street. Originally, there were four more houses, but they degraded and were torn down years before we bought the property. "Is this yard all yours?" one guest asked, staring at the enormous space—"It's amazing!"

I had been in the middle of weeding a section when she and her husband arrived.

I told her it was, and she said, "Why don't you have photos of it in the description?"

Well, she had me there. Why didn't I have pictures of it in the description?!

I immediately added photos of the yard to both listings. In the decade since we purchased the property, we have planted at least twenty fruit trees, dozens of fruiting bushes, perennial herbs, roses, asparagus, hundreds of strawberry plants, and so much more. We have dug and installed a large pond, added a gazebo, and even a playhouse and enclosed trampoline for our children and guests to use. Combined with a dozen brick pathways I've installed over the years, it's a great space to walk around and enjoy. No matter the time of year, something is blooming or growing! As silly as it sounds, I hadn't thought of it as a selling point, but it certainly was, and it took a guest's query to make me think of it.

No slip and slide here—One of the major draws of Cottage West is the vintage claw-foot bathtub prominently displayed in the photos. It was a heck of a find, and I've received many comments on it. However, it's tricky to get in and out of, as one guest kindly let me know in his private feedback. I immediately added an anti-slip mat to the inside of the bathtub. It hangs on the side so that people wanting to take a bath instead of a shower don't have to have it in there if they don't want. I also added a non-slip absorbent bath mat to the outside of the tub. Since then, I've had several guests comment that the bath mats have helped. A win-win!

Even an RV needs this—When installing the curtains for the Hedy Lamarr Airstream, I wasn't thinking about light-blocking curtains. Not at all. I had found the perfect pinup girl fabric in a thin cotton fabric with a cream background. Our décor is cherry red and cream, so it was perfect. Or so I thought. After two guests commented on the early morning sun waking them from their slumbers, I knew it was time for an upgrade. I found another pinup girl fabric, this with a black background, added a lining to make it even more light-proof, and rehung the curtains. Instant success! Guests want to sleep in, especially when they are experiencing a fantastic little getaway in a garden oasis surrounded by a busy city.

Think about the kids—Despite having plenty of children of my own (ages range from 34 years to toddler), I had thought little about children when I opened my first STR, Cottage West. In my defense, my vision for Cottage West was as a writing and artists' retreat. That vision quickly changed as I learned more and more about who my guests were and what they needed. One of our early guests with small children helped me with that glorious private feedback. She wrote glowingly about Cottage West on the public side of things and gently suggested in the private feedback that a Pack 'n Play (playpen) and a high chair be provided.

I immediately brought over both and later added a full set of children's dinnerware (plates, bowls, cups, and plastic silverware) to my offerings. It made sense, and I was thankful for the suggestion since I have seen many positive comments since on how helpful those items have been for traveling families.

Ice, Ice, Baby - Many times, we don't think of things we don't use ourselves. This was never clearer than when I met Denise, a guest who has returned multiple times to Cottage West. One of her children has regular recurring appointments at a local hospital and she tells me that Cottage West feels like home. The third time she visited, it was in the middle of winter, whereas the first two had been during the summer and early fall, when everything was hot outside and a nice, icy drink was necessary. However, in the winter, when it is bone-chillingly cold, I want warm things and the tap water is cold enough, there's no need to add ice to it. I kind of slack off in the winter on refilling the ice trays in Cottage West's freezer. Denise gently suggested I monitor the ice levels in her private feedback.

The next time she visited, she grinned at me and said, "You got a new ice bucket, and it was completely full of ice!"

Guests love it when I respond to their feedback and are pleased as punch when I take their suggestions into account. They feel heard. And that is a powerful thing. Listen to your guests, take what they have to say in, and give them what they want, as much as is humanly, logistically, or financially possible. Doing so will build your business and improve your reviews. Guaranteed.

How to Identify and Avoid Problem Guests

———

You will encounter a steep learning curve as a new host. One of the biggest challenges is trying to avoid, from the beginning, problem guests. The likelihood that you will get them eventually is almost certain. No amount of screening ever seems to be enough. However, the first few guests are the most crucial. In fact, with problem guests (read that - locals who want to party), you are most likely to encounter them in the first few months of your listing. Why? Because it is new (which they can quickly see by looking at your reviews or lack thereof) and they are banking on you being a new host who is too inexperienced to recognize the warning signs.

It should go without saying that the use of your STR as a party house is *not* recommended. But just in case you need some clarification why, I have four huge reasons.

Reason #1 - Most of the listing platforms will toss you off their sites if they found you to be intentionally hosting them. Even those who just screwed up and accepted the wrong folks are suspect. A listing platform will expect you, the host, to do some level of screening on your own.

Reason #2 - It is a quick way to piss off your neighbors and local law enforcement.

Reason #3 - Party house hosts open themselves up to lawsuits and even criminal charges should something happen during the party - think accidental falls, fights, a fire, et cetera. It simply isn't worth it.

Reason #4 - Party houses are the number one reason that Airbnb, VRBO, and other short-term rentals have a bad rap. Don't give the hotels industry, communities, and city leaders any additional ammunition against us.

Now, I suspect that 99.9% or more of my readers have no intention of putting a party house in play, so let's talk about what we can do to avoid hosting parties of any kind.

Close Down for Certain Days

My husband often refers to me in jest as a thrifty, murderous soul. But he isn't far off. As the financial manager of the house, and the mad genius behind our STR journey, I am intent on squeezing as much profit as possible from our STRs. I want them 100% occupied. Standing empty means that we are still paying for heating/cooling, maintenance and more, with zero funds flowing in, so it is a rare day that I will close voluntarily. That said, having experienced the stress of having guests over major "party" holidays, I can tell you it is absolutely worth it to shut down for the following days each year:

- 4th of July

- Halloween

- New Year's Eve

If you live in an area that is popular with the college kids during spring break and you don't want a drunken fistfight love fest going on, I recommend you figure out those dates and block them off on your calendars.

If maintenance is needed, I try to schedule it in advance and shut down for the minimum time needed. I also shut down our STRs for two other days per year, but those are for our own parties. Potluck-style, family-friendly events, which we often invite our neighbors to. No drunken fistfight love fests for us. We are family and kid-friendly and I just want the opportunity to relax on my property without guests. Those three days listed above are definite party days for locals and are absolutely not worth risking my future income, the wrath of my neighbors, or my own elevated stress levels.

Screen Locals with a Sharp Eye

Locals are trouble more often than not. I remember when I started hosting; I saw them degraded plenty on the Facebook STR host groups and thought it was unfair. It was a lesson I had to learn for myself, obviously! Now that I have, I can say with confidence that at least 70% of locals are trouble that you do not want. Why 70%? Well, I've allowed locals and had decent, occasionally superb dealings with them. I accept them on a case-by-case basis at this point. I especially look at what they say and how they say it.

Recent changes have removed the pre-booking message that Airbnb allowed me to automatically ask prior to booking. I basically would ask, "What brings you to Kansas City?" This weeded out most of the locals looking to party. Now, recent changes have taken that option away. However, after a guest has booked, you can still ask the question. If a guest responds in a *way* that concerns you, you have the option to cancel the booking without penalty.

Chances are they *won't* tell you, "I want to party down and trash the shit out of your place." Geez, wouldn't that be nice if they did? But words and phrases used give them away. Here are a couple that have been used on me:

- *"I live in the city, but I just want to chill for a night before heading out on vacation."*

- *"My place doesn't have electricity and I just need a place to stay for the night."*

- *"I want to have a couple of friends over and my roommates aren't cool with that."*

- *"I'm just looking for a chill place for a Friday night."*

The only one that you should consider is the second one, and even if you did, you would be wrong. That second one? Whew! Those were the two couples who *moved their entire apartment in overnight*! Complete with two extra televisions, bric-à-brac, heck, they even *decorated*. It took three hours to get them out past their checkout time and they left their heroin kit behind in the rush.

A recent local guest was a fair to middling kind of guest. Here is what he said when submitting his request:

"Hi Christine! we are not traveling; we are local and having work done at our home. It will be me, my wife, 12-year-old son and our dog Bonnie. The place looks fantastic and cozy. My wife will love the tub."

This was the guest who stayed for two days and their dog ate one rug and scratched holes in another. They never responded to my request for damages, but Airbnb's AirCover gave me compensation. Other than that, they left the house in fair condition. I would chalk this up to simply being a guest who is an irresponsible pet owner. That said, they received a poor review because they had allowed their dog to damage the property and then ignored my request to pay for the damages.

I have been lucky compared to some. This is nothing. A few hundred dollars in replacement costs for a couple of carpets, nothing crazy. Exercise caution, but don't be too cautious. It is a fine edge to walk, but in most cases, use common sense. Then again...

"Common sense is something that everyone needs, few have, and none think they lack." - Benjamin Franklin

Security Cameras - Do's and Don'ts

I strongly recommend that you invest in exterior cameras for your property. We use Ring devices—both doorbells and the motion sensor floodlights with cameras, to ensure our property is safe and that there are no parties or illegal activities taking place.

I've already told you the stories of the guests who tried to move in, but I would like to reiterate that a Ring doorbell simply will not provide you with the security footage you need.

We purchased the motion sensor floodlights, which were then mounted on the roof of the porch, some eight to nine feet up and out of reach. The Ring annual coverage plan includes unlimited devices and costs just $100. This is perfect for small and large properties alike. You can look back through weeks of recordings if necessary. In one case, when I noticed a decorative pillow was missing, I tracked down the footage from when it left the house (under the arm of a guest) and asked them for compensation. They paid for it without complaint.

The Ring cameras also caught our first (and last) New Year's Eve guests firing off a weapon into the air at the stroke of midnight. Comments on what goes up must eventually come down aside, seeing that footage was enough to encourage me to block that day in all future years. I don't need the money that badly.

A couple of things to keep in mind for security cameras and other monitoring devices.

1. Never, EVER, place any of these recording devices *inside* of your property. Even if they are pointed outwards, looking out of a window. You are opening yourself up to litigation and the potential of being banned from the booking platform the complaining guest has booked on. It is far too easy for those cameras to be turned

around so it is now facing inside, a photograph to be taken, and a complaint to be lodged.

2. Disclose all devices on the listing platforms you are using. With Airbnb, this can mean putting it in multiple locations, often along with a brief explanation of *why* it is there.

3. If your security cameras rely on a Wi-Fi connection, I strongly advise you place the Wi-Fi hardware somewhere the guests cannot access. Hosts have mentioned on multiple host groups of ne'er-do-wells disabling the Wi-Fi in order to move in and out of the property without a video record of their movements. If they don't want to stay in a property with exterior recording devices, that's fine, but they shouldn't stay with anyone who has that in place (including nearly all hotels and motels) and expect that they should be able to disable such devices.

4. Be a good host. Don't listen in on your guests' discussions! Give them privacy. If they are hanging out on the front porch, leave them be. Later, if an issue arises, then would be a time to review video footage and audio (yes, hosts have overheard guests planning to make up complaints or steal items from the property and submitted that footage to law enforcement and/or the listing platforms).

One other security device you may wish to consider is a loud noise alert device, like Minut or Noise Aware. These devices can help you stop parties before they begin. You can set them to notify you if the noise inside of the STR rises above a certain level or a certain period. We have a Minut device inside of Cottage West and I highly recommend it.

Like it or not, we live in an increasingly recorded digital age. Use those powers for good.

SHORT-TERM RENTAL SUCCESS

Maximize Profit Without Being Cheap

As a business owner, I walk the fine line between keeping my costs low while maximizing profits—and keeping my guests happy and the reviews glowing.

In one Facebook group I belong to, Airbnb Hosts Automated, I saw a post that read:

"lol just got hit with the 'we ran out of toilet paper' I told them there's a store 3 minutes from the house. Lol I don't even care about reviews anymore."

#1—This host's ratings will be in the toilet soon, if they aren't already.

#2—He is being, as the saying goes, penny-wise and pound-foolish.

And while I saw several posts beneath it proclaiming that guests regularly steal toilet paper (especially in Hawaii where a package of toilet paper can cost $26 or more), I could not disagree more with the original poster. Especially not after he said that his cleaners leave two rolls per bathroom, and this was for a four-day stay! As another host commented, *"Guarantee someone has gotten desperate and no telling what they used then."* I shudder to think.

If you are going to be cheap, go to Dollar Tree and buy things on the cheap there (lint rollers, cough drops, plastic organizers, treats). There are plenty of items that folks don't expect you to supply top of the line. But for crying out loud, give people enough good toilet paper to wipe their butts with the entire time they are there.

Embrace Fun

—

I will start by saying that this isn't always the right approach. It depends on your potential guests and their expectations. If you are, for example, catering to an upscale crowd, or business guests, this might not apply. For the rest? Read on.

Perhaps because I'm a parent and a creative entrepreneur, I love the whimsy and fun that we can put into our STRs. In fact, I specifically seek places that have fun, quirky attractions. The OMG! category of Airbnb is not to be missed. Just click on it under Traveling and look at some of the offerings. They will have some great ideas on making your STR an amazing destination for guests. In fact, when I look at traveling and want to stay somewhere cool, I am usually willing to go to a strange city I have never been just to stay in a weird or unusual place like a giant potato, for example. And I *know* I'm not the only one!

That said, even a run-of-the-mill normal STR can have some fun add-ins. Look at some ideas below...

Chalkboard table—I've mentioned this before, but it bears repeating: a chalkboard table is a lot of fun. I grabbed a bottle of chalkboard paint and painted a couple of layers on a worn table, tossed some chalk in a little glass, and set it out for guests.

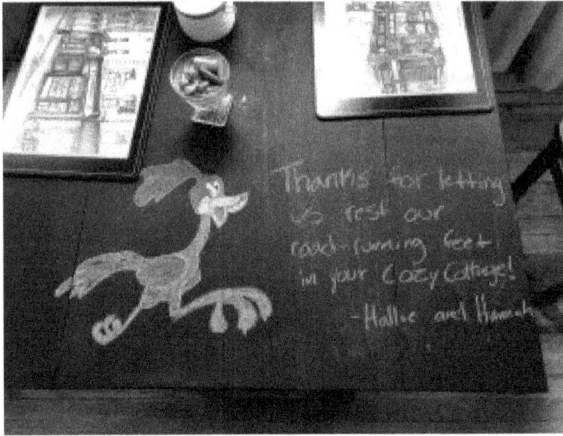

What followed next has been truly magical. Guests love it! For that matter, so do I. And after a friend suggested it, The Cottages Art Spot (@thecottagesart) was added to Instagram. Go check it out!

Guests use this space to tell me they loved their stay (always a nice boost to morale), and they often create gorgeous works of art to add to the Instagram page.

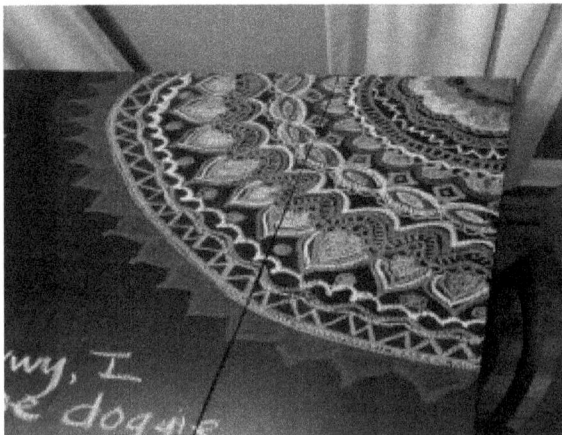

Kids love it, and it keeps them creating art in a safe space; and using something that is temporary (as opposed to using markers on my Tree of Life table) and harmless.

It was such a hit with guests that I added it to our Airstream dinette table as well.

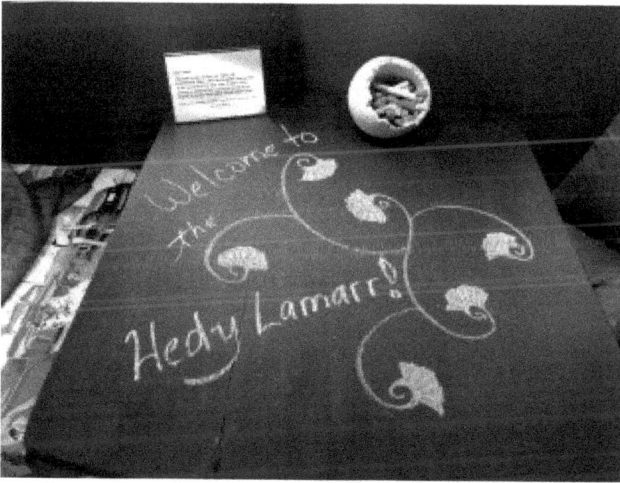

Magnetic words on the fridge—This can get pretty racy, but guests really seem to enjoy it. I take photos of them from time to time. Here are a couple...

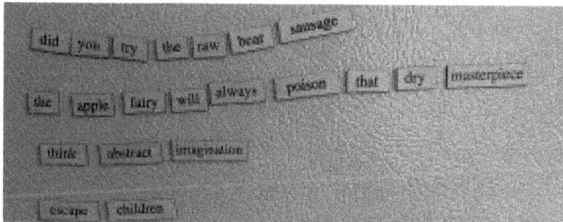

The guests enjoy themselves, and I have a bit of a giggle seeing what they come up with.

<u>Books, books, and more books</u>—As an obsessive reader, and as an author, I'm of the opinion that there are never enough books in the world. I mean, seriously, bring on the books. I collect them from my house, Dollar Tree ($1.25 for a hardcover book? Heck, yeah!), garage sales, etc. It's worth it, especially when I get notes like the one below from Joanna, who wrote *"I took* The Writing Life *by Annie Dillard. Very rarely does a book make me feel something like that one did in that kind of way."* Which is, in essence, the very reason I love to share books with guests.

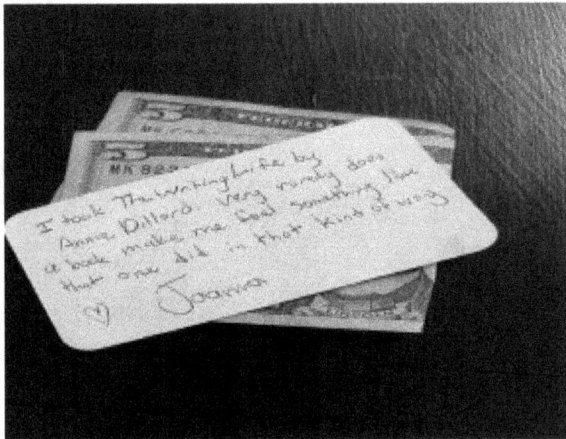

<u>Play Games, All Sorts</u>—That's a quote from Mary Poppins, by the way. Have some games stocked in your STR. Whether it is board games, cards, a Ouija board (why not?!), lawn darts, or even a cool vintage Nintendo—your guests will appreciate your consideration. I also try to leave some fun things for kids (books, Word Find, Sudoku, crossword puzzles and more) as well. Traveling can get tedious, especially if they are road-tripping, and many guests are happy to have a fun distraction while they unwind.

These are just a few ways in which you can make your STR feel special for your guests.

Part IX: The Future

When to Get Out

B uzz kill!

What? Get *out*?

By now, I've hopefully gotten you to the spot where you are ready and raring to go, and now I'm laying this chapter on you? You might think right about now, "But wait! You just spent an entire book getting me ready to operate an STR and now this?"

Yes. Because there will come a day when it is time to move on to other things, retire, return a property back to a long-term rental, sell it, etc.

The Bubble WILL Burst

Nearly every week I see some new article out warning that short-term rentals will soon be history. Certainly, the flood of *unregulated* STRs will be. From towns that flat-out ban them, to neighborhoods up in arms over party houses and parking nightmares in their quiet suburbs. Things are changing by the minute. Increasingly prohibitive controls are being put in place—in my area, throughout the United States, and beyond. In most cases, this is a positive change. I'm seeing more and more areas requiring hosts to get STR licenses with their respective cities and the blessing of their nearby neighbors. While challenging considering the bad press that a handful of STR hosts have provided the media, having the cooperation of your neighbors can be essential to your success in the STR world.

The Need for Quality Housing

I told you at the beginning of this book that I was going to guide you into creating something of unique value for yourself and the guests that you host. I think I have done that. But I would be remiss if I didn't address the elephant in the room, which is the housing situation in our country today.

In the past two years, partly because of COVID, as well as the resulting supply chain issues and financial woes, we have had a surge in property prices and a growing lack of quality long-term rentals.

Landlords who are tired of dealing with low-income, low-quality renters are heading over to the STR side of things. Who can blame them when their income can sometimes be more than twice what a long-term rental can bring with less wear and tear?

"The past is behind,

Learn from it.

The future is ahead,

Prepare for it.

The present is here,

Live it."

- Thomas S. Monson -

Just as there are people looking for unique and personal short-term stays, there are also people who just need a decent place to live. A place that is well-cared for, one in which the owners/landlords provide a well-maintained home for a fair rent. And these places were already hit or miss before the advent of short-term rentals. Now? In some areas, they are a scarcity.

Rental homes have often been rife with poor fixes, poor maintenance, and are often in poor neighborhoods. And along with them, the term 'landlord' has become a derogatory one, one that immediately connotes a money-grabbing slum-lord.

Running an STR will teach you so many things. The art of hospitality, certainly, but also how to be a good human. How to provide a thing of value, and to do it with kindness and empathy. I think those traits can then transfer over to long-term rentals. Not just transfer, but grow into an ethic we can all live with. Fix things when they are broken. Provide a place of value, all in exchange for a fair rental price.

As my husband and I turned our first home into a rental property, it was a simple decision for me in deciding what kind of landlord I would be. I would be the one who fixes things. In ten years, I've had four different tenants. Two were problem tenants—late rent (if at all), shut-off utilities, overgrown grass. The other two have been wonderful. One couple stayed with us for six years and told me once that I was "the best landlord [they] had ever had."

Running an STR can do the same for you. It can teach you to provide a good, welcoming home to another person. Whether they stay for one night or a thousand.

It Makes Financial Sense for Now...

When we purchased Cottage West and began renovating her, the rents in our neighborhood were very low. So low that I would have cleared less than $100 per month above the loan payment I had incurred as part of the full renovation we had done.

Our plan at the time was to renovate it and rent it out with the potential future of living in it ourselves once we retired. The chance to actually make our money back quicker renting it out as an STR was quite appealing, and that is what we did.

A Financial Step up for Other Things

I mentioned in the Preface that choosing to STR can open the door for other things. The book you are holding in your hands is a prime example of that. By making nearly three times the amount of money I did cleaning houses, and over four times the amount it would have made as a long-term rental, our STR allows me to stay home and write.

For many budding authors, they walk the knife's edge of having to provide for themselves (and often their families) and also create something that people will want to read. It takes time to do that; it has a steep learning curve, and the income that our STRs provide has made that road to authorship easier.

What do you dream of doing or creating? Having an STR (or two or more) can allow you the freedom to do whatever your heart dreams of. I know one STR owner who has a handful of properties, outsources her cleanings and the management of the properties, lives in Germany half of the year, and travels the world the other half.

Owning and operating our STRs has allowed me to work from home and become a foster and adoptive mother to two little ones. It also helped me to be a better mother to my children. I'm less stressed, less under the gun to get a ton of things done on the weekends that I would normally be too busy to do on the weekdays. Finally, owning the two houses and two RVs and operating them all as STRs (for hopefully the next decade) will eliminate our mortgage debt in record time, allow us to retire comfortably, and even give us the chance at long-yearned for travel to far-off destinations.

Eventually, though, our kids will be grown and gone. In another twelve years, debt-free, it will be time for us to retire fully. When we do, the properties we have that are actual houses—Cottage West and Cottage East—will convert from STRs back to long-term rentals, giving back to the community these two homes. I'll likely keep the Hedy Lamarr Airstream as a cute little she-shed writing retreat that doubles as a fun place to host occasional friends or family members, and we can either sell the Proud Mary RV or use her to travel the United States.

Be the Landlord You Would Want to Rent From

I've rented some truly awful places in my life. My late teens and early twenties were filled with a variety of challenging locations—aging apartment buildings with a medley of problems and rather unresponsive management. And when I became I homeowner myself, I began to understand the scale of need that a property has. There is no fix it and forget it. Yet many landlords try to do that very thing.

I've watched, with no small amount of frustration, the troubles that our neighbors in an aging apartment building across the street have had with absentee owners who are interested only in the almighty bottom dollar. Recently, the new owners decided that trash pickup was "too expensive" and *canceled their service*, telling the tenants that they would each have to get a contract with the city and pay for their own trash service. For weeks, the trash has been piling up higher and higher, attracting vermin and degrading the property further.

If you own your property, consider a time in the future when you will no longer rent it as an STR, but as a long-term rental instead. Think about the landlord you want to be. Yes, you will still run into the occasional bad tenant. But I'm a firm believer in putting my best foot forward. A good tenant will find you and be thankful that you are a step above the rest.

There are many reasons to plan on getting out of the STR business, just as there are plenty of reasons to be in it. Choose wisely, and with clarity on what your particular needs and goals, and those of your community, are.

The Day After Tomorrow

I'm a huge fan of Joanna Penn, an author and podcaster. And while nearly all of her work is focused on success as an author, Joanna is a futurist. She spends a significant chunk of her time focusing on the question, "What comes next?"

Companies rise and fall thanks to world events often completely outside of our control. Never has this been more evident in our recent history than it was with COVID. We are still struggling with the virus, supply chain issues, and more as a result. Restaurants, the travel industry, even the labor force in general are still reeling from its effects. And now we have rising inflation, and possible imminent recession to work through.

Look to the future, the day after tomorrow if you will, in order to anticipate what comes next. Nothing lasts forever. Keep your finger on the pulse of the market, and a sharp eye on trends, and you will know when to pivot and evolve your business. Whether it is taking it in a unique direction (think of the OMG category on Airbnb) or returning to a long-term rental, or even re-branding your space as an artist's retreat (or something else) - keeping your eye to the future can never hurt.

In Summary

———

I set out to write a book that would give you the basics of becoming a host by:

- Helping you decide if becoming an STR host was for you

- Choosing themes and decor

- Anticipating the needs of pets and children and, of course, all of your guests

- Preparing the space for its first guests

I feel I have done that. I've also reviewed how to deal with guests, what to say and how to say it, and the various ins and outs of running a hospitality-based business.

I hope I have also imbued a sense of ethical business dealings - something often missing in the hype of "make lots of money." We are humans, and fallible. We deal with other humans, whose stories we often know little about. Becoming a successful host is about putting your best foot forward with every guest you host. It's also about keeping a keen eye on your bottom line, recognizing when you may have a problem guest, and dealing with them effectively and efficiently.

It means looking to the future for the next set of trends and rolling with them, evolving, as Airbnb and the other short-term rental platforms have evolved.

I hope I have done all of that for you. Please feel free to email me with questions or comments at shuckchristine@gmail.com. As with my other two non-fiction books, this book is not a static creation. It will evolve, change, and improve based on the thoughts you share with me. What have I not thought of? What could I do better at? What questions have I not answered?

As I answer them, I will update the e-book and paperback versions. Later, likely annually or less often, I will update the hardcover as well.

We live. We learn. We grow.

I look forward to hearing from you. Thank you so much for reading this book. And please don't forget to leave a review on your favorite bookselling platform so that other potential future hosts can know their money will be well spent reading it!

Part X: Additional Resources

STR Co-Host Resources

———

At some point, you may wish to automate your STR business, and co-hosting can be done in several ways. First, you might find a local individual who can handle any or all of the cleanings, guest interactions (messages, etc), maintenance, and supplies for you. Usually this is done with a royalty split. Before I rolled out my first STR, I was the co-host for a neighbor whose STR was less than a block away. I handled the cleanings and some of the guest interactions for a simple 80/20 host/co-host split. Most co-hosts will ask for 20-40% of the gross, depending on what services are being provided. The more you outsource, the more you will pay.

You can also find companies who will handle the hosting for you:

- Vacasa

- Evolve

- Guest Ready

- Pillow

- Senstay

This list is far from complete and remains ever-changing as new companies appear and older ones are taken over or bought out.

Whether choosing to co-host and split the profits, or use a company and pay a flat rate, a careful review of an individual's experience, or a company's consumer reviews, will help you identify the best fit for your needs.

Podcasts and Facebook Groups

———

I have learned so much from a variety of podcasts and host-centric groups on Facebook. While we were deep in the renovations of Cottage West, taking it from an abandoned and deteriorating property to the warm and welcoming STR it is today, I listened to endless podcasts. I wanted to learn as much as possible so that my learning curve was shorter and my mistakes were hopefully not too costly.

Podcasts

My favorite podcasts while I was busy preparing our first STR were *Shampoo & Booze* and *Get Paid for Your Pad*. There is more, plenty more, but those two definitely resonated with me. Here are their links:

Shampoo & Booze—**http://www.shampooandbooze.com**[1]/

Get Paid for Your Pad—**https://getpaidforyourpad.com/podcast-2/**

A few more for you to consider:

Vacation Rental Success: http://www.cottageblogger.com/category/podcast/

Unlocked: http://unlocked.libsyn.com[2]/

Hosting Your Home: http://hostingyourhome.com[3]/

The Property Podcast: http://thepropertyhub.net/podcast/

The Hosting Journey: https://www.thehostingjourney.com/category/podcast/

Sarah and T—https://sarahandt.com[4]/

---

1. http://www.shampooandbooze.com/

2. http://unlocked.libsyn.com/

3. http://hostingyourhome.com/

Those are just a few of the well-known podcasts. I suggest dipping your toes into a nice variety.

Facebook Groups for STR Hosts

I have found that a majority of the contributors on these Facebook pages are not used to running their own businesses and, therefore, decide with hospitality in mind. They allow their emotions to color their experiences with guests and to respond in some truly un-businesslike ways. So, don't take what others advise as gospel—use your own judgment.

Many of the folks there have a ton of experience, and some are truly consummate hosts. They can share little gems that will take your short-term rental to the next level! I am a member of several groups on Facebook that might interest, help, and guide you:

AIRBNB, VRBO, HOUFY, and Book Direct Vacation Rental Professionals

AIRBNB Whole Home Hosts

Airbnb Professional Cleaners

New to STRs, Airbnb, and Hosting

Airbnb Homes for Sale

Airbnb Profit Club

The Hosts of Airbnb Automated

Airbnb Hosts Kansas City

---

4. https://sarahandt.com/

Additional Reading

———

Every Airbnb Host's Tax Guide by Stephen Fishman, J.D.

Get Paid for Your Pad by Jasper Ribbers

Vacation Rental Success by Joel Rasmussen

Make Money on Airbnb by Sally Miller

Part XI: Spreadsheets and Lists

Spreadsheets Detailed

———

Y ou can download copies of all the spreadsheets at my author website: **https://www.christineshuck.com/str-success-resources**. But here are some highlights of it.

My spreadsheet tracks info I find important. You might have other areas you want to track, but here are the data points I have found useful:

- Average occupancy rate (how often is the property booked)

- Average rental income (not the other fees, simply what I'm getting per night at a property)

- Total cleaning fees paid

- Gross income

- Running totals on all costs

- Net income

- Percent of take home (gross income minus costs expressed as a percentage)

- Monthly totals

- Yearly totals

- Income by booking platform

Having this information at my fingertips allows me to predict the ebb and flow of the seasons, plan for the future, and even give detailed information to a potential landlord for rental arbitrage, or a loan officer if I ever decide to expand.

Let's unpack this a bit as we move through the spreadsheets and their examples.

Predicting Income

Starting out, you can compare other properties (closest in proximity and amenities) to yours in order to get a baseline comparison of what you can expect in terms of income. Obviously, this helps you decide in the first place if using your property as an STR rental is worthwhile or not.

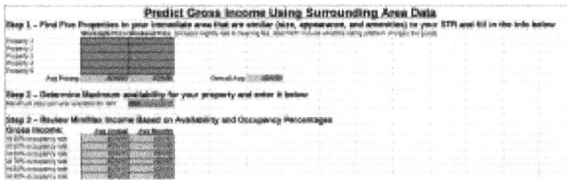

The image above is the spreadsheet you would use, and the image below is the sample that is included to help guide you through using it. You can find step-by-step instructions in the chapter How Much Will I Make? This is in Part I.

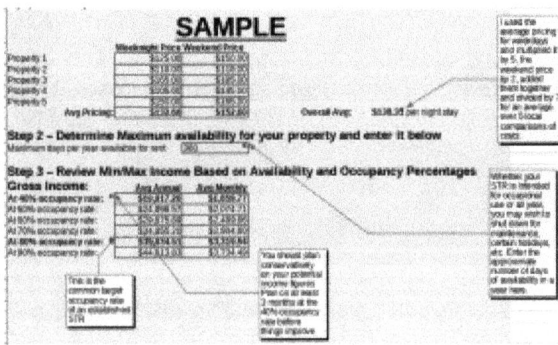

Startup Costs

Startup costs are highly individual and unique to the STR that you are creating. However, I've supplied a basic idea of what my startup costs were for Cottage West in Part II: Anticipating Costs.

Income by Platform

Once you are up and running with your STR, this spreadsheet will probably become one of your "go to" destinations. I regularly update this as bookings come in because, well, I enjoy seeing the numbers grow.

I've added a snapshot of the sample one as well, so you can see some numbers in action. You may see movement in one, possibly two, online platforms at first. However, I urge you to diversify and spread to others. It's never a good idea to put all of your eggs in one basket. Companies go bankrupt, raise or lower in popularity in the rental market, and heaven forbid one decides there is something wrong with your STR and shuts you down completely (whether permanently or for a short few days).

Expense and Income (by Year)

This is one of my favorite worksheets. That probably makes me a complete nerd, but there you go. This allows me to see exactly how much I can expect to make after expenses and the 15% savings I squirrel away for taxes and major repairs.

As expenses occur, you can add them in here, or simply add them all in at the end of the month. I pay myself a set wage of $3,000 per month and put anything above $3,000 in net income into our renovations fund as we work toward completing our other two STR renovations.

I made room for up to three separate properties to be tracked, but you can reduce or expand this for your own needs.

Again, below is the same as above, but with sample numbers in it.

Average Daily Rental Spreadsheet

The average daily rental spreadsheets, which unfold over a year, track several pieces of information. Here is what I track using this spreadsheet:

- Average daily price

- Total nights booked and average occupancy per property

- Occupancy Income (and average occupancy income over a 12-month period)

- Cleaning Income (and average cleaning income over a 12-month period)

- Total Gross Income (adding Occupancy and Cleaning incomes together) and the average gross monthly income

- Percentage of income that comes from cleaning fees

I will not go into detail on every one of these, as they are mostly self-explanatory.

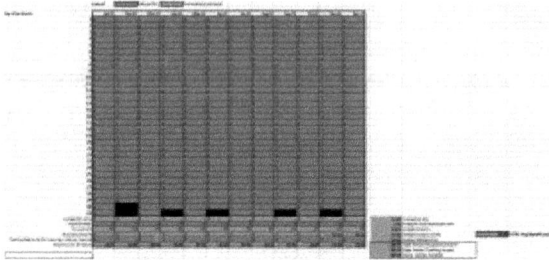

When I compare Cottage West, which is a two-bedroom, one bath house to the Hedy Lamarr, the difference in occupancy rates is significant. Currently, Cottage West has an average occupancy rate of 90.44% for 2021 and an overall 83.02% for 2022. Whereas, the Hedy Lamarr Airstream has a 67.56% average occupancy rate for 2021 and 47.35% for 2022. Post-Covid 2021 showed an explosion of travel, but the now-contracting economy is giving us a different picture of what is coming.

Knowing what the occupancy rate gives me an idea of what I need to improve, but also what to expect in terms of a baseline income. I also know that the Airstream is rather unique. It's different, and it also has its limitations (composting toilet, small shower). While I expect that the occupancy rate will increase with exposure (it had 83 reviews in late 2021 compared to 257 reviews on Cottage West) and time on the market, it will probably never be the high occupancy rate I see with Cottage West.

Average Daily Price

At the end of each month, I take a few minutes to fill in the rates charged on each day at my two STR rentals. Now, if you end up with dozens of rentals, this could be far more time-consuming and simply not make sense. But for a handful? I think it is well worth your time and will allow you to dial in closely after a solid year of data collecting and allow you to expect income better.

As you can see, the prices vary. And not just from day to day, but in certain months. My average occupancy fees vary by as much as $30 per night between January and July.

My personal goal is to have the property occupied one hundred percent of the month. I often play with the pricing and reduce it the closer we get to the open date. If the calendar is still showing a vacancy for Cottage West on the day of, I will manually drop the price from $99 to as low as $51. I'm still getting a $50 cleaning fee for a cleaning that takes me 45 minutes at most, so it is still worth it to me to drop it to that level. If I were not providing most of the cleanings myself, then it definitely would not be worth it to me to adjust the price down so significantly.

Cleaning Income

I am still cleaning Cottage West and the Hedy Lamarr myself. I only outsource these cleanings when I go on vacation. However, in the future, I will want to outsource it. For convenience, because my author business dictates, I spend more time writing, et cetera. When I pull the trigger, I want to know how much income I'll be losing and how much incoming cleaner(s) can expect to make on a monthly basis. I already know that for the year of 2021, I've seen the following income breakdown for Cottage West:

Annual Occupancy Income: $24,405.79

Annual Cleaning Income: $10,575.00

Over 40% of the total income for Cottage West comes from cleaning fees. The Hedy Lamarr, with its $25 cleaning fee looks a little different...

Annual Occupancy Income: $9,126.28

Annual Cleaning Income: $2,850.00

That's just 31% of my total income going to cleaning fees. For the time I take (currently around 1.5 hours for both properties), and my proximity to my two STRs, I would far prefer to hold on to that huge chunk of income. Later, if my writing income were to take off exponentially, it might eventually make more sense to pay cleaners to handle it while I write.

Your Monthly Budget

This is a great tool for forecasting what your monthly and annual budgets might be in the coming years.

I don't use it as often as I do the Expense and Income sheet, but I wanted to give you a standard budget sheet in case you needed it.

SAMPLE

Expenses	Monthly	Annual
Mortgage/Rent		
[Property Name]	$ 585.00	
Annual & Monthly Memberships		
Streaming Service 1	$ 4.00	
Streaming Service 2	$ 10.00	
Streaming Service 3		$ 19.99
Security Monitoring		$ 600.00
Bookkeeping/Financial Software		$ 279.00
Website/Domain Fees		$ 276.00
STR License		$ 271.38
House Insurance		
STR Insurance	$ -	$ 764.00
Management/Cleaning Fees		
Management Fees		$300.00
Cleaning Fees		$300.00
Property Taxes		
Taxes for [property name]		$ 428.14
Repairs Budget		
Repairs	$ -	$ 500.00
Supplies		
Supplies (toilet paper, etc)	$ 50.00	
Utilities		
Electric	$ 200.00	
Gas/Propane	$ 125.00	
Water	$ 25.00	
Trash/Recycling	$ 115.00	
Cell phones	$ 145.00	
Savings and Investments		
Slush Savings for income taxes & NME (25% of STR income)	$ 898.25	
Non-Monthly Expenses [divided by 12] not part of monthly expenses	$ 306.00	
Total Expenses (excluding NME expenses)	$ 2,890.21	
Income		
Average Gross Monthly Income (from Expense and Income – (Year)	$ 4,491.16	
Overage/Shortfall:	$1,600.94	

Profit and Loss

Calculating profit and loss from one year to the next can come in handy as you hone your STR expenses down and your income up. It can also serve as a good predictor of how utility expenses might increase from year to year. In the sample below, you see the utilities costs rose across the board for electric, gas and water. It can help you puzzle out why income is falling, or even if there are any price increases you need to pass along to your guests.

Profit and Loss (by Year)

Again, these spreadsheets are available for download, free of cost, at: **https://www.christineshuck.com/str-success-resources**

Shopping/Stocking Lists

You can find all of the shopping/stocking lists available for free download on my author website at:

https://www.christineshuck.com/str-success-resources

I will update these frequently, but please let me know if a specific link does not work. You can always email me with that information at shuckchristine@gmail.com.

Best wishes for a successful short-term rental business for you and yours!

Don't miss out!

Visit the website below and you can sign up to receive emails whenever Christine D. Shuck publishes a new book. There's no charge and no obligation.

https://books2read.com/r/B-A-BOLF-OVDDC

BOOKS 2 READ

Connecting independent readers to independent writers.

Also by Christine D. Shuck

Benton Security Services
Hired Gun
Smoke and Steel

Chronicles of Liv Rowan
Fate's Highway

Gliese 581g
G581: The Departure
G581: Mars
G581: Earth

War's End
War's End: The Storm
War's End: A Brave New World
Tales of the Collapse
War's End Omnibus - Books 1-3

Standalone

The War on Drugs: An Old Wives Tale
Get Organized, Stay Organized
Winter's Child
Short-Term Rental Success

Watch for more at christineshuck.com.

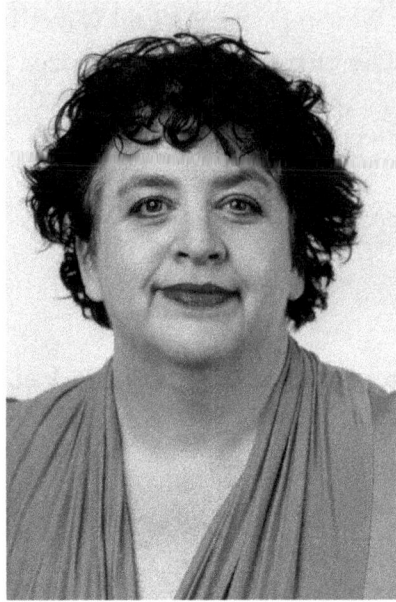

About the Author

Fueled by homemade coffee ice cream, a lifelong love of words, and armed with strong female (and male) characters I cross genres like the Ghostbusters crossed the streams in pursuit of the question.

"What is the question?" you ask.

The question is simple. It asks, "What would you do, if..."

What would you do if you were fifteen years old and the world as you knew it fell apart? Would you run? Would you fight? Would you survive? – Meet Jess and her brother Chris in the *War's End* series.

What would you do if you had a chance to live your life over? Not just once, but twice? – Meet Dean Edmonds in *Fate's Highway*

What would you do if everyone you loved was lost to a terrible virus and you faced the real possibility of the extinction of the human race in the dark void of space? – Meet Daniel Medry in *G581: The Departure*

What would you do if hitmen were after you and you had no idea why? – Meet Lila and Shane in *Hired Gun*

If I don't keep you turning pages late into the night, desperate to know what happens next, then I have failed at my job. I'm a Taurus and born in Missouri. That makes me bull-headed and stubborn to boot. I don't believe in failure or mistakes, only learning opportunities and clever conversation. There's not much I won't do to make you burn the midnight oil reading my words while you suffer sleep-deprivation the following day. It's my secret superpower.

Born in flyover country, I've also lived in Arizona and northern California. I am an eclectic mix of snark and oddball humor. My colorful metaphors would make a fishwife blush. I'm an incompetent gardener, a dreamer and doer, in love with old houses and shooting pool, and chief organizer of all thing's household and financial. Feed me tiramisu and I'm yours forever.

Find me on all major platforms by visiting Linktree: https://linktr.ee/christinedshuck

Read more at christineshuck.com.